# SAVING DINNER THE LOW-CARB WAY

**ALSO BY LEANNE ELY**

Saving Dinner

# SAVING DINNER THE LOW-CARB WAY

**Healthy Menus, Recipes, and the Shopping Lists That Will Keep the Whole Family at the Dinner Table**

## LEANNE ELY

BALLANTINE BOOKS • NEW YORK

A Ballantine Book
Published by The Random House Publishing Group

Copyright © 2005 by Leanne Ely

www.ballantinebooks.com

Cataloging-in-Publication Data is available from the Library of Congress.

ISBN 0-345-47806-1

Manufactured in the United States of America

9 8 7 6 5 4 3 2

First Edition: January 2005

Text design by Helene Berinsky

*This book is dedicated to all the flybabies and Menu-Mailerettes who asked for this book in the first place.*

# CONTENTS

# ACKNOWLEDGMENTS

At the risk of sounding repetitive, I must once again thank and acknowledge many of the same people I thanked in *Saving Dinner*, plus a few more. Please take the time and wade through my moment of gushing. Seriously, every person mentioned goes beyond the call of duty and is a stellar example of integrity, loyalty, and hard work—a rare combination in today's world. Without every one of them, this book would never be in your hands.

First up, Michelle Tessler, my incredible agent. Thank you, Michelle, for continuing to look after me. Then there is my editor at Ballantine, Caroline Sutton. It is so refreshing to work with such a pro. Thank you for your incomparable expertise and attention to detail.

A stalwart example of a true friend and the best dang cheerleader a gal could ask for is Marla Cilley, known throughout the world as the FlyLady. To me, she is just Marla: dear friend, confidante, and a total gift of encouragement. Thank you, Marla, for believing in me before I did! In the same breath, I have to mention Kelly, too. Not only can this girl crack me up, but she thinks like I do, too. Now that's scary!

I would be remiss if I didn't offer one of the biggest thank-yous to my own staff at Menu-Mailer, especially for their work during the months I was writing this book. They really did and continue to do a tremendous job. I am blessed with the best customer-service team anyone could ever ask for: Kandi, Bonnie, and Demaris, thank you for continually going beyond the call of duty. You gals deserve a standing ovation for the dedication and TLC you extend to our subscribers.

The FlyLady staff has become like family: Tom, Dana, Justin, Rebecca, and everyone else down at FlyLady Central. Thanks for your support!

Another big thank-you to the Simply Saving Dinner list on Yahoo.com that shopped, cooked, taste-tested, and evaluated every single recipe in the book. To me, having real families do your recipes is better than any test kitchen in the world.

A special thanks to Bonnie Schroader, who runs the Simply Saving Dinner list on Yahoo groups. She did every single grocery list in this book, kept her copy-editor eyeball on the recipes, and coordinated the test kitchening. Not only that, but she did it all while juggling a move, kids, and the Simply Saving Dinner list! What a woman—thanks Bonnie!

And last, but never least, a huge thank-you to my mom, Miriam, fondly known the world over (thanks to my big mouth) as Muzz. Muzz does all things administrative for Menu-Mailer and keeps me from losing my non-administrative mind. Thanks Muzz . . . you're the absolute best!

# INTRODUCTION

Every time I turn around, it seems something new has appeared, making fabulous low-carb claims, whether it is a book, product, spokesperson, or what have you. The never-ending hit parade of all things low carb doesn't seem to be coming to an end anytime soon. As a matter of fact, the business of low carb is escalating faster than the national deficit—not quite in the trillions of dollars, but definitely billions. For a long time I thought this was just a Dr. Stillman déjà-vu deal, until the flashback wouldn't go away.

As the Dinner Diva of SavingDinner.com, I want to know what my subscribers want. A while back, I began getting hit with a ton of requests for a more low-carb-friendly Menu-Mailer. The last straw came when one of my subscribers who had been with me from the beginning e-mailed me and told me that her husband had been diagnosed with diabetes. And yes, she asked the fatal question: Would I please do a more low-carb-friendly Menu-Mailer?

Like a lot of people, I believed the low-carb fad diets would hit the skids anytime soon, and I couldn't wait. I pooh-poohed the idea and scoffed at the notion of those limiting their carbs. In my mind, eating low carb was eating bacon, eggs, and steaks. You call that healthy?

I did a little research and discovered going low carb didn't need to look like steak for every meal. Quite the contrary—it could be a lifestyle of variety and flavor, could actually contain vegetables, and be outright healthy. In the meantime, I tried going low carb myself.

Not only did I feel better and more satiated, while eating less food, but I began to read and read some more on the actual, real-life, not-manufactured-for-your-viewing-pleasure science. There really is something behind this low-carb phenomenon. It is here to stay, and I'm very glad it is. I guess you could say that I'm a believer.

In August 2003, I realized this was something exciting and introduced my first Low-Carb Menu-Mailer (for more information on Menu-Mailer, go to www.savingdinner.com). I realize now, more than a year later, that low carb isn't a diet; it's a lifestyle and it is here to stay.

It is in that spirit that I offer you the next *Saving Dinner* book. While the recipes are low carb (and that is 10 or fewer net grams of carbs for the entrée—not counting the Serving Suggestions), there are certain members of your household who aren't going to want to do low carb all the way, so there are regular, non-low-carb Serving Suggestions offered as well for that person or persons. You don't have to make two dinners so you can low carb it, while the kids eat a regular, non-low-carb meal. Isn't that great?

Just as the first *Saving Dinner* book offered you the recipes, menus, and shopping lists divvied up by weeks and seasons, so does this book. I think this is the way to go in today's world—having the hard work of menu planning already done and ready to go. The shopping lists are again at your convenience, on my website in a printer-friendly format, just go to www.savingdinner.com and click on Shopping Lists. You don't need to schlep your book to the grocery store and take a chance on losing it.

A big caveat to those who may be following certain low-carb diets with big lists of do's and don'ts. This book does not adhere to any one low-carb diet plan. It's just low carb, end of story. You won't find odd-ball ingredients like pork rinds, weird ketosis-inducing, low-carb mixes made with strange things you've never heard of. I use regular ingredients and admittedly, I've been skewered for it. People have written absolutely unprintable e-mails denouncing my low-carb ideas because I had the audacity to add 1 tablespoon of whole-wheat flour to a recipe—even though I've kept the recipe very low carb. Apparently, in their eyes I've committed the carbinal sin (get it?) by using big no-no ingredients.

But the issue in my mind, is keeping the recipes low carb (they are) and using real ingredients, easily accessible and found at just about any market, to carry out this goal. I've held true to this principle for years: that the more natural and real your ingredients are, the easier it is to accomplish and keep up as a lifestyle.

Consider this book as another weapon in your arsenal to keep you organized and on target to help you get dinner on the table. With this tool, you can accomplish that without having to sacrifice your time, health objectives, or sanity. *Saving Dinner the Low-Carb Way* is all about helping you meet your goals.

# HOW TO USE THIS BOOK

*Saving Dinner the Low-Carb Way* is designed to give you everything you need to do dinner. The recipes, serving suggestions, and, most important, categorized shopping lists are all contained within this book. Speaking of shopping lists, for your convenience, I have also added printer-friendly shopping lists to my website (savingdinner.com) so you can print out the appropriate list without having to lug your book to the store.

There are two types of Serving Suggestions in the book: LC (low carb) and just Serving Suggestions (regular ones for non-low-carbing family members). The Serving Suggestions are asterisked on the grocery lists because I don't want you to feel roped in by any of my suggestions. However, the LC Serving Suggestions are not asterisked, as I am trying to help you put together a complete, low-carb meal.

I would strongly suggest that you read the recipes before you hit the grocery store each week with the list. It helps to know what your menu is about before you head out the door. That five minutes of reading through the menu and recipes may help you make a quick decision if your store is out of something or if you would prefer a substitute. You can't do that if you don't know what you're shopping for!

This book is chock full of sidebars . . . read them! There is a ton of information to help you take full advantage of these menus and to make the recipes your own. As I was writing these recipes out, I would think of something else that would empower you in the kitchen, so I made a sidebar out of it. The more you know, the faster you're able to do the recipes and shopping. That's a good thing!

When appropriate, I have added Do-Ahead Tips to help make dinner easier the next day (e.g., precooking turkey or chicken for a salad, etc.). However, there are all kinds of things you can do the day before, if you so desire. I kept it basic, you might want to do more—it's totally up to you. You also can move days around if you want—just remember that the Do-Ahead Tips may no longer be appropriate if you do.

If you do want to make substitutions (due to allergies, preferences, etc.) on some of the grocery items, feel free! For those who are more kosher minded, the pork and shellfish recipes can easily be substituted out with any poultry, chicken being a very easy fit.

Just remember, *Saving Dinner the Low-Carb Way* is another weapon in your arsenal to help you conquer the drive-thru and keep your family at the dinner table. Enjoy!

# SAVING DINNER THE LOW-CARB WAY

# FALL

# Week One

**DAY ONE:** Sweet Teriyaki Pork Chops

**DAY TWO:** Low-Carb Mexican Casserole

**DAY THREE:** Jack Fish

**DAY FOUR:** Bourbon Chicken on Spinach

**DAY FIVE:** Happy Family Beef Stir-Fry

**DAY SIX:** Crock Goulash

## SHOPPING LIST

### MEAT

4 boneless, skinless chicken breast halves

1 pound beef flank steak

4 boneless pork chops (4–6 ounces each)

1½ pounds boneless pork (cut into 1-inch cubes)

1 pound ground turkey

1 pound cod fillets (if not using frozen, other firm white fish can be used instead)

### CONDIMENTS

olive oil

sesame oil (dark; sometimes called toasted; comes in a small bottle)

teriyaki sauce

soy sauce (low sodium, if available)

ketchup

honey

vinegar

**lc salad dressing—your choice

## PRODUCE

1 small green bell pepper

1 small red bell pepper

½ pound snow-pea pods

2 bunches green onions (you'll need ½ cup + 4 teaspoons)

3 pounds onions (keep on hand)

2 medium tomatoes

1 head garlic

1 piece gingerroot (you'll need 1 tablespoon grated)

1 bag spinach (you'll need 4 cups); **lc (1 meal)

red cabbage (you'll need 3 cups)

**lc 2 heads lettuce (*not* iceberg) (2 meals)

**lc salad veggies (2 meals)

**lc spaghetti squash (1 meal)

**lc green beans (1 meal)

**lc turnip (1 meal)

**lc broccoli (1 meal)

**lc cauliflower (1 meal)

**lc pumpkin wedges (purchase a small pie pumpkin or sugar pumpkin) (1 meal)

**russet potatoes (1 meal)

**red potatoes (2 meals)

## CANNED GOODS

1 14½-ounce can chicken broth (you'll need ½ cup)

1 jar salsa (you'll need ¾ cup)

black olives (you'll need ¼ cup chopped)

apple juice (you'll need 4 tablespoons, if not using bourbon)

**black beans

**SPICES**
garlic powder
basil
paprika
caraway seed

**DAIRY/DAIRY CASE**
butter
half-and-half (you'll need ½ cup)
sour cream (you'll need 4 tablespoons + ½ cup)
Cheddar cheese (you'll need 1 cup shredded)
Monterey Jack cheese (you'll need ½ cup shredded)
**lc 8-ounce package cream cheese

**DRY GOODS**
whole-wheat flour
sugar
cornstarch
1 package taco seasoning mix
**2 pounds brown rice

**FROZEN FOODS**
1 pound cod fillets (if not using fresh)

**BAKERY**
**lc low-carb tortillas

**OTHER**
bourbon (you'll need 4 tablespoons, if not using apple juice)

*Serves 4*

*1 tablespoon olive oil*
*1 small green bell pepper, cut into strips*
*¼ cup teriyaki sauce*
*1 tablespoon honey*
*1 tablespoon vinegar*
*½ teaspoon garlic powder*
*4 boneless pork chops*

In a skillet, heat olive oil over medium heat. Add bell pepper and sauté till crisp-tender. Turn on the broiler.

In a small bowl combine the teriyaki sauce, honey, vinegar, and garlic powder, mixing well. Place pork chops in a broiler-safe pan, and puncture all over with a fork (go easy—you aren't trying to ventilate the thing). Then evenly drizzle teriyaki mixture over the top of the chops. Give it a few minutes to marinate a bit (finish making the rest of your dinner). Broil 6 inches from the heat for about 5 minutes on each side, depending on the thickness of your chops. Make sure you watch them under the heat—you don't want them turning into shoe leather.

PER SERVING
202 Calories; 8g Fat (37.6% calories from fat); 22g Protein; 10g Carbohydrate; 1g Dietary Fiber; 51mg Cholesterol; 733mg Sodium. Exchanges: 0 Grain (Starch); 3 Lean Meat; 1 Vegetable; ½ Fat; ½ Other Carbohydrates.

LC SERVING SUGGESTIONS: Serve with sautéed green beans (see sidebar on page 251) and Turnip Fries (page 248).

SERVING SUGGESTION: Add brown rice.

# LOW-CARB MEXICAN CASSEROLE

*Serves 4*

1 pound ground turkey

1 package taco seasoning mix (or 2 tablespoons of my homemade
   taco seasoning blend; see sidebar)

½ cup chopped green onion, divided

¾ cup salsa

1 cup shredded Cheddar cheese

¼ cup chopped black olives

4 tablespoons sour cream

In a skillet, over medium-high heat, cook turkey. Stir in seasoning mix and remove from heat. Preheat oven to 375 degrees F.

Spread cooked turkey mixture in the bottom of an 8-inch-square baking dish. Sprinkle ½ the green onions over the turkey and top with salsa, then sprinkle cheese over top. Bake for 10 to 15 minutes or until cheese is bubbling and hot. Garnish with the rest of the green onions, olives, and a blob of sour cream.

**PER SERVING**
368 Calories; 23g Fat (56.7% calories from fat); 29g Protein; 11g Carbohydrate; 2g Dietary Fiber; 126mg Cholesterol; 1172mg Sodium. Exchanges: 3½ Lean Meat; ½ Vegetable; 0 Fruit; 0 Non-Fat Milk; 2 Fat; ½ Other Carbohydrates.

**LC SERVING SUGGESTIONS:** Make taco-chips from low-carb tortillas. You want the equivalent of 1 tortilla per person. Add a big green salad, and you're set.

**SERVING SUGGESTION:** Add some black beans.

---

## HOMEMADE TACO SEASONING

🍁 The ready-made stuff in the markets can be filled to overflowing with MSG and other stuff you may not want. Here is a quick recipe for making your own:

   1 cup dried minced onion
   ⅓ cup chili powder
   2 tablespoons cumin
      (personally, I add another
      tablespoon of cumin. Love
      it!)
   4 teaspoons red pepper flakes
   1 tablespoon oregano
   4 teaspoons garlic powder
   2 teaspoons onion powder

   Mix everything together and keep in a sealed container.

# JACK FISH

*1 pound cod fillets, thawed if necessary*
*Salt and pepper to taste*
*2 medium tomatoes, chopped*
*4 teaspoons green onion, chopped*
*½ teaspoon basil*
*2 teaspoons butter*
*½ cup shredded Monterey Jack cheese*

Preheat oven to 450 degrees F. Place fish fillets in lightly greased baking dish. Sprinkle fish with salt and pepper. In a bowl, combine tomato, onion, and basil; spoon over fish.

Dot fish with butter. Bake for about 8 to 10 minutes or until fish flakes easily when tested with a fork. Turn off the oven. Sprinkle fish with cheese and return to oven just to melt the cheese.

**PER SERVING**
160 Calories; 5g Fat (30.0% calories from fat); 24g Protein; 3g Carbohydrate; 1g Dietary Fiber; 61mg Cholesterol; 143mg Sodium. Exchanges: 0 Grain (Starch); 3 Lean Meat; ½ Vegetable; ½ Fat.

**LC SERVING SUGGESTIONS:** Serve with Mashed Faux-tay-toes (page 246) and steamed broccoli.

**SERVING SUGGESTION:** Add baked potatoes.

# BOURBON CHICKEN ON SPINACH

*Serves 4*

*4 boneless, skinless chicken breast halves*
*Salt and pepper to taste*
*1 tablespoon whole-wheat flour, for dusting*
*1 tablespoon olive oil*
*4 cloves garlic, pressed*
*1 small onion, chopped*
*4 tablespoons bourbon (can substitute apple juice for bourbon)*
*½ cup chicken broth*
*½ cup half-and-half*
*4 cups spinach*

Season the chicken with salt and pepper and dust in flour. In a skillet, heat the olive oil over medium-high heat and sauté chicken until browned and cooked through. Remove chicken from the pan and keep warm. Turn the heat to medium.

Add the garlic and onion to the pan and cook till tender, but don't let garlic brown. Add the bourbon and cook another minute. Now add chicken broth and half-and-half and reduce until slightly thickened, about 2 to 3 minutes or so. Be careful not to let boil too vigorously, or sauce will break.

Return the chicken to the sauce to reheat.

Place 1 cup spinach on each plate, and carefully add chicken on top. Pour sauce evenly over the top. The heat from the chicken and sauce will perfectly wilt the spinach.

PER SERVING
266 Calories; 9g Fat (34.2% calories from fat); 30g Protein; 7g Carbohydrate; 2g Dietary Fiber; 80mg Cholesterol; 210mg Sodium. Exchanges: 0 Grain (Starch); 4 Lean Meat; 1 Vegetable; 0 Non-Fat Milk; 1½ Fat.

LC SERVING SUGGESTION: Serve with Baked Pumpkin Wedges (page 252).

SERVING SUGGESTION: Add baked red potatoes.

# HAPPY FAMILY BEEF STIR-FRY

2 tablespoons low-sodium soy sauce

4 teaspoons dark sesame oil, divided

1 teaspoon sugar

1 teaspoon cornstarch

1 pound beef flank steak, cut into strips

1 small red bell pepper, cut into strips

½ pound snow-pea pods, julienned

2 cloves garlic, pressed

1 tablespoon gingerroot, grated

In a large bowl, combine soy sauce, half of the sesame oil, sugar, and cornstarch and mix till blended well. Add beef and toss to coat well.

Heat remaining oil in a wok or large skillet over medium-high heat.

Add the bell pepper and snow peas and stir-fry for 2 minutes. Add garlic and ginger, cooking for about 15 seconds. You don't want it to burn.

Remove the bell peppers and snow peas. Now add the beef and stir-fry half the beef at a time, about 3 minutes each batch.

Add back the vegetables to the beef in the pan and toss together to heat.

**PER SERVING**
272 Calories; 15g Fat (50.5% calories from fat); 24g Protein; 9g Carbohydrate; 2g Dietary Fiber; 57mg Cholesterol; 371mg Sodium. Exchanges: 0 Grain (Starch); 3 Lean Meat; 1½ Vegetable; 1 Fat; 0 Other Carbohydrates.

**LC SERVING SUGGESTIONS:** Serve on a bed of spaghetti squash. Add a big green salad.

**SERVING SUGGESTION:** Add brown rice.

# CROCK GOULASH

1 tablespoon olive oil
1½ pounds boneless pork, cut into 1-inch cubes
Salt and pepper to taste
2 medium onions, halved, thinly sliced
¼ cup water
3 cups red cabbage, shredded
3 squirts of ketchup (about 3 tablespoons' worth)
1 tablespoon paprika
1 clove garlic, pressed
2 tablespoons whole-wheat flour
½ cup sour cream
½ teaspoon caraway seed

In a skillet, heat olive oil over medium-high heat. Add pork cubes to the skillet and sauté till browned; salt and pepper to taste. Add the onion and sauté a minute longer. Now add the pork and onion to the Crock-Pot. Add the water to the skillet and get up all the browned bits. Add this to the crock. Add the cabbage into the crock and toss well with the pork.

In a small bowl, mix together the ketchup, paprika, and garlic. Pour over the top and mix well into the pork mixture. Cover and cook on low for 7 to 8 hours, depending on the type of slow cooker you have, or until pork is cooked and tender.

In another bowl, combine flour, sour cream, and caraway seed. Stir into pork mixture and blend thoroughly. Let it cook a few minutes in the crock while you prepare the rest of the meal.

**PER SERVING**
219 Calories; 9g Fat (38.3% calories from fat); 22g Protein; 11g Carbohydrate; 2g Dietary Fiber; 60mg Cholesterol; 147mg Sodium. Exchanges: 0 Grain (Starch); 3 Lean Meat; 1 Vegetable; 0 Non-Fat Milk; 1 Fat; 0 Other Carbohydrates.

**LC SERVING SUGGESTION:** Serve with a big spinach salad. That's all you really need.

**SERVING SUGGESTION:** Add boiled red potatoes.

## Week Two

**DAY ONE:** Low-Carb Crab Cakes

**DAY TWO:** Classic Salisbury Steak

**DAY THREE:** Indian Summer Skillet Chicken

**DAY FOUR:** Dill Salmon Chowder

**DAY FIVE:** Apricot Dijon Pork Chops

**DAY SIX:** Crock Beef Stew with Oven-Roasted Vegetables

### SHOPPING LIST

**MEAT**

4 boneless, skinless chicken breasts

1 pound extra-lean ground beef

1¾ pounds beef stew meat

4 pork chops (about ½ inch thick)

2 cups crab, shredded (if not using frozen or canned)

**CONDIMENTS**

mayonnaise

Dijon mustard

Tabasco sauce

olive oil

vegetable oil

horseradish

cider vinegar

vinegar (if not using white wine)

apricot spreadable fruit/jam (you'll need ¼ cup)

**lc salad dressing—your favorite

## PRODUCE

2 heads garlic

3-pound bag onions (keep on hand)

green onions

celery

2 tomatoes (you'll need ½ cup diced)

4 plum tomatoes

mushrooms (you'll need 3 cups + 12 medium mushrooms)

1 turnip **lc extra (1 meal)

**lc 1 head lettuce (*not* iceberg) (1 meal)

**lc 2 bags spinach leaves (2 meals)

**lc 1 bag coleslaw mix (1 meal)

**lc salad vegetables (1 meal)

**lc broccoli (1 meal)

**lc 3 heads cauliflower (3 meals)

**lc artichokes (1 meal)

**russet potatoes (4 meals)

**lc green beans (1 meal)

## CANNED GOODS

2 cups crab, shredded (if not using frozen or fresh; about 3 6-ounce cans)

2 cups cooked salmon (2 small cans or 1 large can)

2 14½-ounce cans beef broth

1 14½-ounce can chicken broth (you'll need ⅓ cup)

## SPICES

8 basil leaves, fresh

dill

thyme

## DAIRY/DAIRY CASE

2 eggs

butter

half-and-half (you'll need 1½ cups or 12 ounces)

**lc 2 8-ounce packages cream cheese

**lc Cheddar cheese, shredded

**milk

## DRY GOODS

flour

cornstarch

**1 pound brown rice

## FROZEN FOODS

2 cups crab, shredded (if not using fresh or canned)

## BAKERY

1 loaf whole-wheat low-carb bread (you'll need 4–6 slices)

**4 hamburger buns

**whole-grain rolls

## OTHER

white wine (you'll need ¼ cup, if not using white grape juice/vinegar)

white grape juice (you'll need ¼ cup, if not using white wine)

# LOW-CARB CRAB CAKES

*Serves 4*

2 cups crab, shredded (fresh, frozen, or canned)
1 cup soft whole-wheat bread crumbs (or use low-carb bread)
½ cup minced green onion
⅛ cup celery, minced
3 tablespoons mayonnaise
1 egg, beaten
Dash of Tabasco sauce
Salt and pepper to taste
Flour, for dusting
3 tablespoons vegetable oil

In a bowl, combine all ingredients except the flour and oil.

Shape crab mixture into 4 nice cakes, about ¾ inch thick. Dust lightly with flour. In a skillet, heat the oil over medium-high heat. Sauté the crab cakes in the skillet on both sides for about 10 minutes or until golden brown.

PER SERVING
275 Calories; 21g Fat (68.6% calories from fat); 15g Protein; 7g Carbohydrate; 2g Dietary Fiber; 92mg Cholesterol; 350mg Sodium. Exchanges: ½ Grain (Starch); 2 Lean Meat; 0 Vegetable; 3 Fat.

LC SERVING SUGGESTIONS: Serve with a side of Basic Coleslaw (page 255) and some Turnip Fries (page 248).

SERVING SUGGESTIONS: Serve on a bun and with Real Oven Fries (see page 249).

# CLASSIC SALISBURY STEAK

*Serves 4*

1 pound extra-lean ground beef

1 onion, finely chopped

2 tablespoons dry whole-wheat bread crumbs (just toast some bread and crumble)

1 egg, slightly beaten

1 tablespoon horseradish

Salt and pepper to taste

1 tablespoon vegetable oil, divided

1 can beef broth

3 cups mushrooms, sliced

2 tablespoons cold water

2 teaspoons cornstarch

In medium bowl, combine first 6 ingredients, mixing lightly but thoroughly, then shape into 4 oval ½-inch-thick patties.

In a skillet over medium heat, heat oil until hot and place patties in the skillet. Cook about 7 to 8 minutes or until no longer pink and the juices run clear, turning just once. Remove patties from skillet and keep warm.

In the same skillet, sauté mushrooms till soft. Remove mushrooms and add broth, using a wire whisk to scrape up the browned bits off the bottom of the pan. Allow broth to simmer till slightly reduced. Mix cornstarch with cold water, mixing well till combined (no lumps!). Add to broth mixture and cook over medium heat (it needs to simmer) for 3 to 5 minutes or until thickened. Add back the mushrooms and stir well, serving the mushroom gravy over patties.

**PER SERVING**
358 Calories; 24g Fat (59.7% calories from fat); 24g Protein; 12g Carbohydrate; 1g Dietary Fiber; 79mg Cholesterol; 381mg Sodium. Exchanges: ½ Grain (Starch); 3 Lean Meat; 1 Vegetable; 3 Fat; 0 Other Carbohydrates.

**LC SERVING SUGGESTIONS:** Serve with Mashed Faux-tay-toes (page 246) and steamed broccoli.

**SERVING SUGGESTION:** Use regular mashed potatoes, too.

# INDIAN SUMMER SKILLET CHICKEN

*Serves 4*

4 boneless, skinless chicken breast halves
Salt and pepper to taste
1 tablespoon flour, for dusting
1 tablespoon olive oil, divided
1 onion, chopped
4 garlic cloves, pressed
¼ cup white wine
½ cup tomatoes, diced
⅓ cup chicken broth
8 fresh basil leaves, chopped (remove stems)

Season the chicken with salt and pepper and dust lightly in flour (you truly don't need much).

In a skillet, heat half the olive oil over medium-high heat. Sauté the chicken and brown on both sides, about 4 minutes each side. Remove from pan and keep warm.

Add remaining olive oil and heat, then add the onion and garlic in the pan; sauté until the onion is translucent. Add the white wine and then, using a wire whisk, deglaze the pan (scraping up the browned bits from the bottom of the pan). Now add the tomatoes and chicken broth. Allow the sauce to simmer and reduce the sauce to the desired consistency.

Last, add the basil to the sauce and return the chicken to the pan to heat. Serve chicken with sauce over the top.

**PER SERVING**
200 Calories; 5g Fat (24.8% calories from fat); 29g Protein; 6g Carbohydrate; 1g Dietary Fiber; 68mg Cholesterol; 144mg Sodium. Exchanges: 0 Grain (Starch); 4 Lean Meat; 1 Vegetable; ½ Fat.

**LC SERVING SUGGESTIONS:** Serve with a big spinach salad and sautéed green beans (see sidebar on page 251).

**SERVING SUGGESTION:** Add brown rice.

# DILL SALMON CHOWDER

*1 large onion, chopped*
*½ cup celery, chopped*
*½ turnip, chopped*
*3 tablespoons butter*
*1 tablespoon cornstarch*
*½ cup cold water*
*1½ cups half-and-half*
*2 cups cooked salmon (2 small cans or 1 large can)*
*Salt and pepper to taste*
*2 teaspoons dried dill*

In a saucepan, sauté onion, celery, and turnip in butter until lightly browned.

Stir cornstarch into about ½ cup of cold water and add to onion mix. Turn up the heat to thicken, but don't let it scorch; watch it. Add the half-and-half, salmon, salt and pepper to taste, and the dill and heat till nearly boiling and slightly thick; serve.

**PER SERVING**
389 Calories; 26g Fat (60.7% calories from fat); 26g Protein; 11g Carbohydrate; 1g Dietary Fiber; 120mg Cholesterol; 781mg Sodium. Exchanges: ½ Grain (Starch); 2½ Lean Meat; ½ Vegetable; ½ Non-Fat Milk; 4 Fat.

LC SERVING SUGGESTION: A big green salad.

SERVING SUGGESTION: Add whole-grain rolls.

# APRICOT DIJON PORK CHOPS

*Serves 4*

*2 tablespoons butter, divided*
*4 pork chops, ½ inch thick*
*Salt and pepper to taste*
*¼ cup apricot spreadable fruit*
*4 sliced green onions*
*⅛ cup Dijon mustard*
*1 tablespoon cider vinegar*

In a skillet, melt 1 tablespoon butter over medium-high heat, add pork chops, salt and pepper to taste, then sauté for about 4 minutes on each side or until cooked through, depending on thickness of chops. Remove chops from pan and keep warm. Now add the remaining tablespoon of butter, the jam, onion, mustard, and vinegar to pan. Bring to a boil, lower the heat, and simmer 3 to 4 minutes, covered. Add chops back into the sauce and heat through thoroughly. Serve with sauce on top of chops.

**PER SERVING**
305 Calories; 19g Fat (57.2% calories from fat); 24g Protein; 10g Carbohydrate; 1g Dietary Fiber; 84mg Cholesterol; 104mg Sodium. Exchanges: 0 Grain (Starch); 3½ Lean Meat; 0 Vegetable; 2 Fat; ½ Other Carbohydrates.

**LC SERVING SUGGESTIONS:** Serve with steamed artichokes and Baked Cheesy Cauliflower (see page 247).

**SERVING SUGGESTION:** Add baked potatoes.

# CROCK BEEF STEW WITH OVEN-ROASTED VEGETABLES

*Serves 4*

*1 tablespoon olive oil*
*1¾ pounds beef stew meat*
*3 cloves garlic, pressed*
*Salt and pepper to taste*
*1 can beef broth (13–14½ ounces)*
*2 teaspoons thyme*
*12 medium mushrooms*
*4 plum tomatoes, quartered*
*2 onions, quartered*
*1½ tablespoons olive oil*
*1 tablespoon cornstarch, dissolved in 2 tablespoons cold water*

In a skillet, heat ½ tablespoon olive oil over medium heat until hot. Add beef and garlic and brown, salting and peppering to taste. Stir in broth and dried thyme. Bring to a boil and transfer to a Crock-Pot. Cook on high for 4 to 5 hours or on low for 6 to 8 hours, depending on the type of slow cooker you have.

Meanwhile, preheat your oven to 425 degrees F. Lightly grease a jelly-roll pan with a little olive oil. Place the veggies on the pan. Drizzle ½ tablespoon olive oil over vegetables, tossing to coat. Roast in oven for 20 to 25 minutes or until tender.

At the last hour of cooking, add the cornstarch mixture; cook and stir 2 minutes with the lid off or until sauce is slightly thickened and bubbly. Stir in the roasted vegetables and serve.

**PER SERVING**
289 Calories; 13g Fat (39.7% calories from fat); 32g Protein; 12g Carbohydrate; 2g Dietary Fiber; 77mg Cholesterol; 285mg Sodium. Exchanges: 0 Grain (Starch); 4 Lean Meat; 2 Vegetable; 0 Fruit; 1 Fat.

**LC SERVING SUGGESTIONS:** Serve with Mashed Faux-tay-toes (page 246) and Sautéed Garlicky Spinach (on page 253).

**SERVING SUGGESTION:** Serve with mashed potatoes.

# Week Three

DAY ONE: Roasted Chicken and Peppers

DAY TWO: Cream of Butternut Bisque

DAY THREE: Seared Scallops with a White Wine Sauce

DAY FOUR: Cajun Chops

DAY FIVE: Mediterranean Turkey Skillet

DAY SIX: No-Hurry Crock Curry

## SHOPPING LIST

### MEAT

4 chicken breasts

4 pork chops (about ½ inch thick)

1½ cups turkey breast, cooked

1 pound lean beef (to cut into 1-inch cubes)

1 pound scallops

### CONDIMENTS

olive oil

lemon juice

vinegar (if not using white wine)

**lc salad dressing—your choice

### PRODUCE

1 red onion

3-pound bag onions (keep on hand)

1 head garlic

gingerroot (you'll need 2 teaspoons grated)

3 red bell peppers

1 butternut squash (you'll need 1¾ cups chopped)

2 leeks

1 bunch cilantro

**lc 2 bags spinach (2 meals)

**lc 1 bunch Swiss chard (1 meal)

**lc 1 head lettuce (*not* iceberg) (1 meal)

**lc salad vegetables (1 meal)

**lc green beans (1 meal)

**lc 1 head cauliflower (1 meal)

**lc broccoli (1 meal)

**lc rutabagas (1 meal)

**lc spaghetti squash (1 meal)

**lc Hubbard squash (1 meal)

**lc kale (1 meal)

**russet potatoes (2 meals)

**sweet potatoes (1 meal)

## CANNED GOODS

2 14½-ounce cans chicken broth

black olives (you'll need 2 tablespoons sliced)

tomato puree (you'll need 4 ounces)

1 can artichoke hearts (you'll need 1 cup, if not using frozen) Note: *not* from a jar; you do *not* want pre-seasoned.

## SPICES

paprika

onion powder

garlic powder

rosemary

sage

thyme

nutmeg

curry powder

cayenne pepper

white pepper

### DAIRY/DAIRY CASE

butter; **extra

half-and-half (you'll need 1 cup)

1 small package plain non-fat yogurt

**lc 8-ounce package cream cheese

**milk

### DRY GOODS

flour

**1 bag pasta

**1 pound brown rice

### FROZEN FOODS

frozen artichoke hearts (you'll need 1 cup, if not using
    canned)

green peas (you'll need ½ cup)

### BAKERY

**whole-grain rolls

### OTHER

dry white wine (you'll need ⅓ cup, if not using white grape
    juice)

white grape juice (you'll need ⅓ cup, if not using white
    wine)

# ROASTED CHICKEN AND PEPPERS

*Serves 4*

*4 chicken breasts*
*2 tablespoons olive oil*
*1 teaspoon rosemary, crushed*
*1 tablespoon lemon juice*
*Salt and pepper to taste*
*1 red onion, sliced*
*1 red bell pepper, cut into strips*

Preheat oven to 500 degrees F (yes, you read that right). Adjust the oven racks before it heats up. You want the rack in the center of the oven or, at least, in the bottom third if you can't get it centered (so your chicken will roast evenly).

In a large zipper-topped plastic bag, add all ingredients and mush around to thoroughly mix. Let sit on the countertop while you wait for the oven to heat up.

Once the oven has heated, place the contents of the bag into a stainless steel baking pan, arranging the chicken bone side down and not touching. I prefer to use metal when cooking with such high heat.

Cook for 10 minutes, then turn the chicken over. Cook another 10 minutes and the chicken is done. The veggies should be nice and browned. Serve with veggies scooped over the top.

**PER SERVING**
579 Calories; 34g Fat (53.5% calories from fat); 61g Protein; 5g Carbohydrate; 1g Dietary Fiber; 186mg Cholesterol; 184mg Sodium. Exchanges: 0 Grain (Starch); 8½ Lean Meat; ½ Vegetable; 0 Fruit; 1½ Fat.

**LC SERVING SUGGESTIONS:** Serve with sautéed green beans (see sidebar on page 251) and Mashed Faux-tay-toes (page 246).

**SERVING SUGGESTION:** Serve with mashed potatoes.

# CREAM OF BUTTERNUT BISQUE

*Serves 4*

1 teaspoon butter
1 small onion, chopped
1¾ cups butternut squash, peeled and chopped
1 14½-ounce can chicken broth
½ teaspoon nutmeg
⅛ teaspoon white pepper
¾ cup half-and-half

In a saucepan over medium heat, melt butter. Add onion and cook till onion is translucent.

Add butternut squash to onion and cook just a minute. Now add the chicken broth, turn up the heat, and bring to a boil. Reduce heat to low and let simmer (covered) till squash is tender, about 15 to 20 minutes.

Mash or process the squash to desired consistency. (If you like your soup really smooth, you can puree it in batches in a food processor or blender, but if you like a little more texture, use a potato masher.)

Add squash back to saucepan (if you used your blender or processor), then add the spices and half-and-half and bring soup almost to boiling point (but don't boil it, or you will curdle the soup). Serve hot.

**PER SERVING**
117 Calories; 7g Fat (49.5% calories from fat); 4g Protein; 12g Carbohydrate; 2g Dietary Fiber; 19mg Cholesterol; 222mg Sodium. Exchanges: ½ Grain (Starch); 0 Lean Meat; ½ Vegetable; 0 Non-Fat Milk; 1½ Fat.

**LC SERVING SUGGESTION:** Serve with a big spinach salad.

**SERVING SUGGESTION:** Add whole-grain rolls.

# SEARED SCALLOPS WITH
# A WHITE WINE SAUCE

*1 tablespoon olive oil, divided*
*2 leeks, sliced thin, white parts only*
*2 cloves garlic, pressed*
*1 pound scallops*
*1 tablespoon flour, for dusting*
*Salt and pepper to taste*
*⅓ cup dry white wine (or use white grape juice and a splash of*
  *vinegar)*
*1 tablespoon butter*
*¼ cup half-and-half*

In a skillet, heat half the olive oil over medium-high heat. Add the leek and garlic and cook till translucent, about 5 minutes. Remove from pan.

Dust the scallops with the flour, and salt and pepper them to taste. Heat remaining oil in the skillet and cook until nicely browned, about 3 minutes each side. Remove scallops and place with garlic and leeks, and turn up the heat on the pan. Add the wine to the skillet and, using a wire whisk, get all the browned bits up off the bottom of the pan. Cook for just a minute to allow the liquid to reduce slightly. Add the butter to the sauce and finally the half-and-half. Reduce the heat and allow to thicken, but do not boil or the sauce will break. Keep it just under a simmer. Add the scallop-and-leek mixture back into the sauce. Serve.

**PER SERVING**
225 Calories; 9g Fat (38.5% calories from fat); 20g Protein; 12g Carbohydrate; 2g Dietary Fiber; 51mg Cholesterol; 228mg Sodium. Exchanges: 0 Grain (Starch); 2½ Lean Meat; 1½ Vegetable; 0 Non-Fat Milk; 1½ Fat.

**LC SERVING SUGGESTION:** Serve on a bed of spaghetti squash and some braised kale (see sidebar on page 254).

**SERVING SUGGESTION:** Serve on a bed of pasta.

# CAJUN CHOPS

*Serves 4*

1 tablespoon paprika
½ teaspoon onion powder
1 teaspoon rubbed sage
½ teaspoon cayenne pepper
Salt and pepper to taste (about ½ teaspoon each)
½ teaspoon garlic powder
4 pork chops, ½ inch thick
1 teaspoon butter
1 teaspoon olive oil

In a small bowl, combine seasonings. Sprinkle one side of chops heavily with spice mixture. Heat butter over high heat just until it starts to brown. Put chops in pan, reduce heat to medium. Fry on both sides until dark brown, a total of 6 to 8 minutes.

In a skillet, heat butter and oil together over medium-high heat. Add chops, spiced side down. Turn heat down to medium. Add the spices to the other side of the chops while in the pan. Cook on till nicely browned, about 4 minutes on each side.

**PER SERVING**
182 Calories; 9g Fat (46.6% calories from fat); 22g Protein; 2g Carbohydrate; 1g Dietary Fiber; 69mg Cholesterol; 48mg Sodium. Exchanges: 0 Grain (Starch); 3 Lean Meat; ½ Fat.

LC SERVING SUGGESTIONS: Serve with Oven-Roasted Rutabagas (page 249) and steamed broccoli.

SERVING SUGGESTION: Add Real Oven Fries (page 249).

# MEDITERRANEAN TURKEY SKILLET

*Serves 4*

1 tablespoon olive oil
½ cup diced onion
½ cup diced red bell pepper
1⅓ garlic cloves, minced
1 cup frozen artichoke hearts, thawed (or canned)
2 tablespoons sliced ripe olives
1½ cups chicken broth
Salt and pepper to taste
½ teaspoon paprika
½ teaspoon thyme
1½ cups cooked turkey breast, chopped
½ cup frozen green peas, thawed

Heat olive oil in a skillet over medium heat. Add onion, bell pepper, and garlic and cook till onion is translucent. Add artichoke hearts and olives, cooking for 2 minutes. Add broth, salt and pepper, thyme, and paprika and bring to a boil. Cover, reduce heat, and allow to simmer for about 15 minutes.

Stir in the turkey and peas and heat for about 3 minutes, then serve.

**PER SERVING**
184 Calories; 7g Fat (35% calories from fat); 20g Protein; 11g Carbohydrate; 5g Dietary Fiber; 40mg Cholesterol; 422mg Sodium. Exchanges: 0 Grain (Starch); 2½ Lean Meat; 1½ Vegetable; 0 Fruit; ½ Fat.

**LC SERVING SUGGESTIONS:** Serve on a bed of raw spinach. The heat from the turkey will perfectly wilt the spinach. Add a green salad on the side.

**SERVING SUGGESTION:** Add a baked sweet potato.

# NO-HURRY CROCK CURRY

*Serves 4*

*1 pound lean beef, cut in 1-inch cubes*
*Salt and pepper to taste*
*2 teaspoons curry powder*
*1 tablespoon olive oil*
*4 cloves garlic, pressed*
*1 onion, chopped*
*1 small red bell pepper, chopped*
*½ cup water*
*2 teaspoons gingerroot, grated*
*2 teaspoons paprika*
*¼ cup tomato puree*
*¼ cup cilantro, chopped*
*½ cup plain non-fat yogurt*

In a zipper-topped plastic bag, place the beef, salt and pepper, and curry powder. Mush it around to thoroughly coat. For best results, do this step the night before and place bag in refrigerator to marinate. Otherwise, complete this step at least an hour before preparing the dish.

In a skillet, heat the olive oil over medium-high heat. Add the beef and sauté till nicely browned. Add to the Crock-Pot. Now add garlic, onion, and red bell pepper to the skillet and sauté till onion is translucent; add this mixture to the Crock-Pot. Throw ½ cup of water into the skillet and deglaze the pan with your whisk. Get up all the bits and cook for a bit; now add this to the Crock-Pot, too. You are done with the skillet.

To the Crock-Pot, now add gingerroot, paprika, and tomato puree. Cook on high 4 to 6 hours or on low 7 to 8 hours, depending on the type of slow cooker you have. Remember: Not all slow cookers are the same—some cook hotter than others.

Serve in bowls topped with yogurt and cilantro.

**PER SERVING**
329 Calories; 20g Fat (55.0% calories from fat); 26g Protein; 12g Carbohydrate; 2g Dietary Fiber; 70mg Cholesterol; 306mg Sodium. Exchanges: 0 Grain (Starch); 3 Lean Meat; 1 Vegetable; 0 Non-Fat Milk; 2 Fat.

**LC SERVING SUGGESTIONS:** Serve with braised Swiss chard (see sidebar on page 254) and baked Hubbard squash.

**SERVING SUGGESTION:** Add brown rice.

## CARB CALCULATOR

So what is the difference between total carbs and net carbs? A lot! First off, your total carb count reflects everything, including the indigestible, not-going-to-affect-your-blood-sugar, fiber. So while the total count is a concern, it's the **net** count that *really* counts because the fiber *doesn't* count! Got that?

Here's how it works: In the nutritional info on a recipe, you will see two figures you need to know to figure this out: the carb count and the fiber count. It's just a matter of figuring out the difference—literally. Take the total carb count (let's say it is 12 grams) and subtract out the fiber (let's say that's 4 grams), then the **net** carbs per serving will be 8 grams and not 12. The math is easy: 12 − 8 = 4. Get it? Big difference in the two.

So remember, to figure net carbs, just do the math!

**Week Four**

DAY ONE: Easy Skillet Pork Stew

DAY TWO: Buffalo Chicken Breasts

DAY THREE: Ginger-Lime Salmon

DAY FOUR: Animal Burgers

DAY FIVE: Sesame Shrimp

DAY SIX: Crock Morock Chicken

## SHOPPING LIST

### MEAT

1 pound lean pork

4 boneless, skinless chicken breast halves

8 skinless chicken thighs

1 pound extra-lean ground beef

4 salmon fillets (about 6 ounces each)

### CONDIMENTS

olive oil

vegetable oil

sesame oil

Dijon mustard

honey

low-sodium soy sauce

Tabasco sauce

blue cheese salad dressing (you'll need 4 tablespoons)

**lc salad dressing—your choice

**lc mayonnaise

### PRODUCE

3 pounds onions (keep on hand)

2 bunches green onions

2 heads garlic

1 piece gingerroot (you'll need 2 tablespoons)

1 large tomato

1 Granny Smith apple

2 lemons (you'll need 3 tablespoons juice)

2–3 limes (you'll need ¼ cup juice)

1 head iceberg lettuce

mushrooms (you'll need 1 cup)

2 cups green beans

**lc snow-pea pods (1 meal)

**lc celery (1 meal)

**lc 2 heads cauliflower (2 meals)

**lc 1 head lettuce (*not* iceberg) (1 meal)

**lc 1 bunch kale (1 meal)

**lc 1 bag coleslaw mix (2 meals)

**lc salad vegetables (1 meal)

**lc spaghetti squash (1 meal)

**lc pumpkin wedges (1 meal)

**lc turnips (1 meal)

**russet potatoes (4 meals)

CANNED GOODS

apple juice (you'll need ¼ cup)

1 14½-ounce can chicken broth

SPICES

cumin

paprika

thyme

garlic powder

sesame seeds

cayenne pepper

**DAIRY/DAIRY CASE**

low-fat Cheddar cheese (you'll need 2 ounces sliced)

\*\*lc 8-ounce package cream cheese

\*\*milk

\*\*butter

\*\*sour cream

**DRY GOODS**

flour

brown sugar

\*\*2 pounds brown rice

**FROZEN FOODS**

1 pound frozen medium shrimp (buy pre-cooked)

# EASY SKILLET PORK STEW

*Serves 4*

*1 pound lean pork, cut into 1-inch cubes*
*1 tablespoon flour, for dusting*
*Salt and pepper to taste*
*1 tablespoon olive oil, divided*
*1 onion, chopped*
*2 cloves garlic, pressed*
*1 Granny Smith apple, peeled and quartered*
*¼ cup apple juice*
*¾ cup chicken broth*
*2 teaspoons Dijon mustard*
*½ teaspoon thyme*

Dust pork with flour, and salt and pepper to taste.

In a skillet, heat half the olive oil over medium-high heat. Add the onion, garlic, and apples and sauté till onion is translucent. Scrape onion mixture into a medium-size bowl.

Heat remaining oil and brown the pork evenly all over; add pork to the onion mixture once browned.

To the skillet, add apple juice and chicken broth and, using a whisk, scrape up all the browned bits off the bottom. Stir in the mustard and thyme and incorporate well. Add the pork and onion mixture to the skillet and bring to a boil. Reduce the heat and simmer stew for about 15 minutes, stirring as needed.

**PER SERVING**
171 Calories; 8g Fat (41.3% calories from fat); 14g Protein; 11g Carbohydrate; 1g Dietary Fiber; 41mg Cholesterol; 229mg Sodium. Exchanges: 0 Grain (Starch); 2 Lean Meat; ½ Vegetable; ½ Fruit; ½ Fat; 0 Other Carbohydrates.

**LC SERVING SUGGESTIONS:** Serve with Mashed Faux-tay-toes (page 246) and braised kale (see sidebar on page 254).

**SERVING SUGGESTION:** Add mashed potatoes.

# BUFFALO CHICKEN BREASTS

*Serves 4*

4 boneless, skinless chicken breast halves
2 teaspoons butter, melted
1 teaspoon Tabasco sauce
Salt and pepper to taste
2 teaspoons olive oil
4 tablespoons blue cheese salad dressing

In a zipper-topped plastic bag, toss chicken breasts together with melted butter, Tabasco sauce, and salt and pepper to taste.

In a skillet, heat olive oil over medium-high heat. Add chicken breasts and cook till well browned and cooked on both sides.

Serve chicken breast with a tablespoon of cold blue cheese dressing over the top.

**PER SERVING**
244 Calories; 14g Fat (51.2% calories from fat); 28g Protein; 1g Carbohydrate; 0g Dietary Fiber; 83mg Cholesterol; 269mg Sodium. Exchanges: 0 Grain (Starch); 4 Lean Meat; 0 Vegetable; 2½ Fat.

**LC SERVING SUGGESTION:** Serve with Basic Coleslaw (page 255) and celery sticks.

**SERVING SUGGESTION:** Add a baked potato.

# GINGER-LIME SALMON

*Serves 4*

> *4 salmon fillets, about 6 ounces each*
> *¼ cup lime juice*
> *1 tablespoon honey*
> *2 tablespoons gingerroot, grated*
> *2 tablespoons green onions, chopped and divided*
> *4 cloves garlic, pressed*
> *1 tablespoon soy sauce*

In a large zipper-topped plastic bag, add all ingredients together (except for half the green onions). Allow to marinate in the fridge while you get the rest of your dinner together.

Preheat the broiler and lightly grease a broiling pan. Place fish on the pan and cook about 10 minutes or until it flakes with a fork. Sprinkle with remaining green onions and serve.

**PER SERVING**
227 Calories; 6g Fat (23.9% calories from fat); 35g Protein; 8g Carbohydrate; trace Dietary Fiber; 88mg Cholesterol; 373mg Sodium. Exchanges: 5 Lean Meat; ½ Vegetable; 0 Fruit; ½ Other Carbohydrates.

**LC SERVING SUGGESTION:** Serve with sautéed snow peas.

**SERVING SUGGESTION:** Add brown rice.

# ANIMAL BURGERS

*Serves 4*

*1 pound extra-lean ground beef*
*1 teaspoon garlic powder*
*Salt and pepper to taste*
*2 ounces low-fat Cheddar cheese, sliced*
*1 head iceberg lettuce, cut in chunks*
*4 slices tomato*
*1 onion, sliced*

Divvy hamburger into 4 nice patties. Sprinkle garlic powder and salt and pepper on both sides. Preheat broiler.

Place burgers on a broiler pan and cook about 5 inches away from the heat. Cook for about 3 to 5 minutes on each side, depending on how well done you like it. Remember to watch your burgers though and don't get sidetracked, or they will turn into charcoal briquettes just as quick as you don't want them to.

When burgers are finished broiling, blot a little grease from the top of the burgers with a paper towel, then place thin slices of cheese on top. Return to broiler for about 15 seconds, just enough to melt.

Cut iceberg lettuce into huge hunks. These hunks of lettuce are going to be the "buns." Place the burger in between the hunks of lettuce with tomato and onion (and any other condiments you'd like) and chow down.

PER SERVING
363 Calories; 24g Fat (60.1% calories from fat); 27g Protein; 9g Carbohydrate; 3g Dietary Fiber; 91mg Cholesterol; 174mg Sodium. Exchanges: 0 Grain (Starch); 3½ Lean Meat; 1½ Vegetable; 2½ Fat.

LC SERVING SUGGESTIONS: Serve with Turnip Fries (page 248) and Basic Coleslaw (page 255).

SERVING SUGGESTION: Add Real Oven Fries (page 249).

# SESAME SHRIMP

*Serves 4*

1 tablespoon vegetable oil, divided
5 cloves garlic, pressed
1 cup mushrooms, sliced
¼ cup low-sodium soy sauce
2 tablespoons sesame oil
1 tablespoon brown sugar
2 tablespoons toasted sesame seeds
1 bunch green onions, chopped
1 pound frozen medium shrimp, thawed (buy already cooked)
2 cups green beans, steamed

In a skillet or wok, heat half the oil over medium-high heat, then add the garlic and mushrooms. Sauté for 3 to 4 minutes. Now add the soy sauce, sesame oil, brown sugar, toasted sesame seeds, and green onions. Simmer for 3 to 5 minutes. Add green beans and shrimp to the sauce and cook for another 5 to 8 minutes.

**PER SERVING**
280 Calories; 14g Fat (45.6% calories from fat); 26g Protein; 12g Carbohydrate; 3g Dietary Fiber; 173mg Cholesterol; 776mg Sodium. Exchanges: 0 Grain (Starch); 3½ Lean Meat; 1½ Vegetable; 2½ Fat; 0 Other Carbohydrates.

**SERVING SUGGESTIONS:** Serve on a bed of spaghetti squash with a big green salad on the side.

**LC SERVING SUGGESTION:** Add brown rice.

# CROCK MOROCK CHICKEN

*Serves 4*

*8 skinless chicken thighs*
*¼ cup olive oil, divided*
*Salt and pepper to taste*
*4 cloves garlic, pressed*
*3 tablespoons lemon juice*
*2 teaspoons cumin*
*2 teaspoons paprika*
*⅛ teaspoon cayenne pepper*

In a zipper-topped plastic bag, add all ingredients, minus 1 tablespoon of the olive oil, mushing everything together in the bag. Allow to marinate at least an hour, though completing this step the night before will yield better results.

In a skillet, heat 1 tablespoon of the olive oil over medium-high heat. Brown the chicken well on all sides. Throw the browned chicken into the Crock-Pot and add the remaining marinade from the bag.

Cook on low for 7 to 8 hours or on high for 4 to 6 hours, depending on the type of slow cooker you have.

PER SERVING
298 Calories; 19g Fat (58.5% calories from fat); 28g Protein; 3g Carbohydrate; trace Dietary Fiber; 115mg Cholesterol; 121mg Sodium. Exchanges: 0 Grain (Starch); 4 Lean Meat; 0 Vegetable; 0 Fruit; 3 Fat.

LC SERVING SUGGESTIONS: Serve with Spiced Cauliflower (page 246) and Baked Pumpkin Wedges (page 252).

SERVING SUGGESTION: Add baked potatoes.

## Week Five

DAY ONE: Roasted Tomato Soup

DAY TWO: Turkey Deli Wraps

DAY THREE: Korean Stir-Fry Beef and Spinach

DAY FOUR: Herbed Skillet Chicken

DAY FIVE: Sicilian Fish

DAY SIX: Crock Carnitas

### SHOPPING LIST

**MEAT**

1 pound beef round-tip steak

4 boneless, skinless chicken breast halves

1 pound pork shoulder

8 ounces turkey slices

4 fish fillets

**lc ham (for chef's salad)

**CONDIMENTS**

olive oil

vegetable oil

hoisin sauce

low-sodium soy sauce

dark sesame oil

vinegar-based reduced-calorie Caesar salad dressing

**lc salad dressing—your choice

**PRODUCE**

3 pounds onions (keep on hand)

2 bunches green onions

1 head garlic

1 bunch parsley (garnish)

½ pound mushrooms

8 medium tomatoes; **lc 8 extra

8 cherry tomatoes

2 bags spinach

1 head romaine lettuce; **lc (1 head)

**lc 1 bunch kale (1 meal)

**lc spaghetti squash (1 meal)

**lc 1 head lettuce (*not* iceberg) (1 meal)

**lc 1 head cauliflower (1 meal)

**lc broccoli (1 meal)

**lc salad greens (1 meal)

**lc green beans (1 meal)

**lc cilantro

**1 avocado

**russet potatoes (2 meals)

## CANNED GOODS

2 14½-ounce cans chicken broth

1 large jar marinated artichoke hearts (or 2 small jars; you'll
    need 8 hearts)

**lc 1 jar salsa

**black beans (1 meal)

## SPICES

basil

cumin

oregano

thyme

cinnamon

garlic powder

onion powder

crushed red pepper

## DAIRY/DAIRY CASE

heavy cream (you'll need ¾ cup); **lc ¾ cup extra

Parmesan cheese, freshly grated (you'll need 4 tablespoons)

**lc cheese—your choice (for chef's salad)

**lc 8-ounce package cream cheese

**lc 1 egg (you'll need to hard boil)

**lc sour cream (2 meals)

**butter (topping)

## DRY GOODS

cornstarch

**1 package spaghetti noodles

## BAKERY

**lc low-carb tortillas (2 meals)

**whole-wheat-flour tortillas

**whole-grain rolls

**whole-wheat pita bread

# ROASTED TOMATO SOUP

*Serves 4*

8 medium tomatoes
Olive oil
Pinch of salt
1 cup chicken broth
¾ cup heavy cream
½ teaspoon thyme

Preheat oven to 200 degrees F. Core tomatoes and rub the outsides with a little olive oil. Sprinkle some salt in the center. Place the tomatoes on a jelly-roll pan and roast for approximately 4 hours. The tomatoes won't be burned, but browned. Refrigerate till ready to use. Can be frozen, also.

Or, to do it the fast way: Preheat the oven to 425 degrees F and follow the same directions as above. Watch the tomatoes carefully. When they are nice and browned (about 20 minutes, depending on the size of the tomatoes), they are done.

Peel the skin off the roasted tomatoes. In a blender, add the remaining ingredients and process till you get the texture you like. Pour soup into a saucepan and heat till nearly boiling. Serve nice and hot.

**PER SERVING**
216 Calories; 18g Fat (69.8% calories from fat); 4g Protein; 13g Carbohydrate; 3g Dietary Fiber; 61mg Cholesterol; 230mg Sodium. Exchanges: 0 Grain (Starch); 0 Lean Meat; 2 Vegetable; 0 Non-Fat Milk; 3½ Fat.

**LC SERVING SUGGESTIONS:** Serve with a mini–chef's salad: Load a bowl of chopped romaine with chopped hard-boiled egg, ham, turkey, and pieces of cheese. Toss together and serve with the soup.

**SERVING SUGGESTION:** Add some whole-grain rolls.

**NOTE:** If doing the LC Serving Suggestion for tomorrow, DOUBLE this recipe.

# TURKEY DELI WRAPS

*4 cups spinach, shredded*
*4 tablespoons Parmesan cheese, freshly grated*
*4 chopped green onions*
*2 tablespoons vinegar-based reduced-calorie Caesar salad dressing*
*4 romaine lettuce leaves*
*8 ounces turkey slices*
*8 marinated artichoke hearts, drained and chopped*
*Salt and pepper to taste*

In a medium bowl, combine spinach, cheese, green onion, and salad dressing.

Arrange 1 cup mixture over each romaine lettuce leaf. Top each with a portion of turkey, 2 chopped artichoke hearts, and salt and pepper to taste.

Roll up like a burrito and enjoy.

**PER SERVING**
181 Calories; 9g Fat (44.6% calories from fat); 18g Protein; 7g Carbohydrate; 3g Dietary Fiber; 27mg Cholesterol; 1184mg Sodium. Exchanges: 2 Lean Meat; 1 Vegetable; 0 Fruit; 1½ Fat.

**LC SERVING SUGGESTIONS:** Serve with leftover soup from last night and salad made from more romaine lettuce. You can also use low-carb tortillas if you like, instead of the romaine leaves. Just add those carbs into your count.

**SERVING SUGGESTIONS:** Wrap your wrap in whole-wheat pita bread and follow the rest of the suggestions.

**46** ❧ SAVING DINNER THE LOW-CARB WAY

# KOREAN STIR-FRY
# BEEF AND SPINACH

*Serves 4*

1 pound beef round-tip steak, cut into strips
1 tablespoon vegetable oil
1 10-ounce package fresh spinach, stems removed and thinly sliced
Pinch of cinnamon
¼ cup green onions, sliced

### MARINADE

¼ cup hoisin sauce
2 tablespoons reduced-sodium soy sauce
1 tablespoon water
2 teaspoons dark sesame oil
2 large clove garlic, crushed
¼ teaspoon red pepper, crushed

Combine marinade ingredients; pour half over beef. Cover and marinate in refrigerator 10 minutes. Reserve remaining marinade.

Remove beef from marinade; discard marinade.

In a wok or skillet, heat oil over medium-high heat until hot. Add beef (half at a time) and stir-fry 1 to 2 minutes or until outside surface is no longer pink. (Do not overcook.) Remove from skillet with slotted spoon; keep warm.

In same skillet, combine spinach, cinnamon, green onions, and reserved marinade; cook until the spinach is wilted and everything is heated through, stirring occasionally. Return beef to skillet and mix together carefully.

### PER SERVING

262 Calories; 10g Fat (36.2% calories from fat); 29g Protein; 12g Carbohydrate; 3g Dietary Fiber; 72mg Cholesterol; 666mg Sodium. Exchanges: 0 Grain (Starch); 3½ Lean Meat; 1 Vegetable; ½ Fat; ½ Other Carbohydrates.

**LC SERVING SUGGESTION:** Serve on a bed of spaghetti squash with a big green salad on the side.

**SERVING SUGGESTION:** Serve on a bed of spaghetti noodles instead.

# HERBED SKILLET CHICKEN

*Serves 4*

*1 tablespoon olive oil*
*4 boneless, skinless chicken breast halves*
*½ teaspoon thyme*
*1 teaspoon garlic powder*
*Salt and pepper to taste*
*½ cup chicken broth*
*1 tablespoon cornstarch*
*1 tablespoon water*
*2 tablespoons parsley, chopped*

In a skillet, heat olive oil over medium heat. Add chicken and cook 10 minutes or until slightly browned, turning once. Combine the thyme, garlic powder, and salt and pepper and sprinkle over the chicken. Remove the chicken from the skillet and keep warm.

Add the chicken broth to the skillet and, using a wire whisk, scrape the pan and get up all the browned bits. Bring the broth to a boil, add the chicken back in, reduce the heat, cover, and simmer for about 10 to 20 minutes, depending on how big and thick your chicken is.

Remove the chicken again from the skillet and keep warm. Now turn up the heat on the skillet and mix the cornstarch with an equal amount of cold water and mix with a fork into a very smooth paste. Add this mixture to the skillet, using your whisk to blend. Simmer the sauce till nicely thickened. Serve chicken with sauce over the top. Sprinkle parsley over the top of the sauce as a garnish.

**PER SERVING**
166 Calories; 5g Fat (28.6% calories from fat); 28g Protein; trace Carbohydrate; trace Dietary Fiber; 68mg Cholesterol; 173mg Sodium. Exchanges: 0 Grain (Starch); 4 Lean Meat; 0 Vegetable; ½ Fat.

**LC SERVING SUGGESTIONS:** Serve with Mashed Faux-tay-toes (page 246), steamed broccoli, and some baked Hubbard squash.

**SERVING SUGGESTION:** Add mashed potatoes.

# SICILIAN FISH

*Serves 4*

    *1 tablespoon olive oil*
    *4 fish fillets*
    *Salt and pepper to taste*
    *¼ cup water*
    *1 small onion, chopped*
    *½ pound mushrooms, sliced*
    *8 cherry tomatoes, cut in half*
    *½ teaspoon oregano*
    *½ teaspoon basil*

In a skillet, heat olive oil over medium-high heat. Add fish fillets, and salt and pepper to taste. Cook 2 to 5 minutes on each side, depending on the thickness of the fish. Carefully remove fish from skillet and keep warm.

Add ¼ cup water to the skillet and deglaze pan using a wire whisk. Now add the onion, mushrooms, cherry tomatoes, oregano, basil, and salt and pepper again, and cook till tender and onion is translucent, about 5 minutes.

Serve fish with this mixture over the top.

**PER SERVING**
252 Calories; 5g Fat (19.4% calories from fat); 43g Protein; 7g Carbohydrate; 2g Dietary Fiber; 99mg Cholesterol; 131mg Sodium. Exchanges: 0 Grain (Starch); 5½ Lean Meat; 1½ Vegetable; ½ Fat.

LC SERVING SUGGESTIONS: Serve with braised kale (see sidebar on page 254) and sautéed green beans (see sidebar on page 251).

SERVING SUGGESTION: Add baked potatoes.

# CROCK CARNITAS

*1 tablespoon olive oil*
*1 pound pork shoulder, cut into 1-inch cubes*
*Salt and pepper to taste*
*1 teaspoon garlic powder*
*1 teaspoon onion powder*
*1 teaspoon cumin*

In a skillet, heat the olive oil and brown the pork. Add salt and pepper to taste.

Transfer everything to a Crock-Pot and add the spices, mixing well.

Cook on high for 4 to 6 hours, or on low for 7 to 8 hours, depending on the type of slow cooker you have. Pork is ready when it shreds easily using two forks.

**PER SERVING**
237 Calories; 19g Fat (72.5% calories from fat); 15g Protein; 1g Carbohydrate; trace Dietary Fiber; 60mg Cholesterol; 57mg Sodium. Exchanges: 0 Grain (Starch); 2 Lean Meat; 2½ Fat.

**LC SERVING SUGGESTIONS:** Serve with low-carb tortillas or romaine lettuce leaves for wraps. Add chopped cilantro, salsa, sour cream, and sliced avocado.

**SERVING SUGGESTIONS:** Add whole-wheat-flour tortillas and some black beans on the side.

**50** ❊ SAVING DINNER THE LOW-CARB WAY

## A BUNCH OF CROCK

🍂 Unfortunately, not all Crock-Pots or slow cookers are created equal. Depending on the size, age, shape, the temperature it cooks on (some cook hotter, some cooler, but I haven't seen one that tells you what the temperatures are!) and the brand, your results can vary significantly. In addition, the degree to which your slow cooker is filled will also affect your results. As a rule, they should be at least half filled, or, better yet, three-quarters of the way filled up. For our purposes, a smaller pot would be better, like a 3-quart size.

I really wish the manufacturers would have a big convention and standardize the thing for our convenience. Wouldn't that be great? Then we wouldn't have to have this discussion. But suppose you didn't have a slow cooker and had no intention of buying one. Here is a conversion chart of sorts, to use your oven instead. Keep in mind, though, that given all the variables mentioned above, your mileage may vary.

Conventional Cooking Time: 15 to 30 minutes
Crock-Pot Cooking Time: 1½ hours on HIGH; 4 to 8 hours on LOW
Conventional Cooking Time: 30 to 40 minutes
Crock-Pot Cooking Time: 3 to 4 hours on HIGH; 6 to 10 hours on LOW
Conventional Cooking Time: 50 minutes to 3 hours
Crock-Pot Cooking Time: 4 to 6 hours on HIGH; 8 to 18 hours on LOW

Most stews, pot roasts, and other uncooked meat/poultry and vegetable combinations will require at least 8 hours on LOW or 4 to 6 hours on HIGH.

**DAY ONE:** Low-Carb Shake-and-Bake Chicken

**DAY TWO:** French Onion Soup

**DAY THREE:** Seared Salmon with Lemon Sauce

**DAY FOUR:** Peggy's Southwest Crustless Quiche

**DAY FIVE:** Asian Pork Stir-Fry

**DAY SIX:** Crock Roast with a Red Wine Sauce

## SHOPPING LIST

**MEAT**

4 chicken breasts (with skin and bone)

4 salmon fillets

8 ounces cooked turkey breast, skinless

1 pound boneless pork (use the butt or loin, etc.)

1½ pounds chuck roast

**CONDIMENTS**

olive oil

vinegar (if not using red wine or sherry)

balsamic vinegar

low-sodium soy sauce

Dijon mustard **lc extra

**lc salad dressing—your favorite

**PRODUCE**

3 pounds onions (keep on hand)

1 lemon

1 head garlic

12 ounces fresh snow-pea pods

12 medium mushrooms

**lc 1 bag spinach leaves (1 meal)

**lc 1 head lettuce (*not* iceberg) (1 meal)
**lc 1 head red cabbage (1 meal)
**lc 2 heads cauliflower (2 meals)
**lc 2 heads broccoli (2 meals)
**lc salad vegetables (1 meal)
**lc spaghetti squash (1 meal)
**lc green beans (1 meal)
**baby carrots (1 meal)
**cherry tomatoes (1 meal)
**russet potatoes (1 meal)
**red potatoes (1 meal)

## CANNED GOODS

1 4-ounce can green chili peppers
1 jar salsa (you'll need ½ cup)
3 14½-ounce cans beef broth
1 14½-ounce can chicken broth

## SPICES

bay leaf
thyme
paprika
nutmeg
ginger powder
garlic powder
onion powder
black pepper
cayenne pepper

## DAIRY/DAIRY CASE

butter
5 eggs
4 ounces half-and-half

Swiss cheese (you'll need 1 cup)

Cheddar cheese (you'll need 2 ounces or ½ cup); **lc extra

**lc 8-ounce package cream cheese

**milk

**DRY GOODS**

whole-wheat flour

brown sugar

cornstarch

wheat germ (you'll need 2 tablespoons)

croutons (you'll need ⅓ cup)

**1 pound brown rice

**BAKERY**

**whole-grain rolls

**OTHER**

red wine (you'll need 1¼ cups, if not using red grape juice)

red grape juice (you'll need 1¼ cups + 1 teaspoon, if not using red wine)

sherry (you'll need 1 teaspoon)—optional

# LOW-CARB SHAKE-
# AND-BAKE CHICKEN

*Serves 4*

*⅓ cup whole-wheat flour*
*Salt and pepper to taste*
*1 teaspoon thyme*
*1 teaspoon paprika*
*1 teaspoon garlic powder*
*1 teaspoon onion powder*
*¼ teaspoon cayenne pepper*
*4 chicken breasts (with skin and bone)*

In a large zipper-topped plastic bag, add the flour and seasonings and shake well to combine. Preheat oven to 400 degrees F.

Add the chicken to the bag, 2 pieces at a time. Lightly shake to coat.

Now put the chicken on a lightly greased baking sheet and bake for about 30 minutes or so, depending on the size of the chicken breasts. After 20 minutes in the oven, turn the chicken over to finish cooking on the other side.

PER SERVING
540 Calories; 27g Fat (46.3% calories from fat); 62g Protein; 9g Carbohydrate; 2g Dietary Fiber; 186mg Cholesterol; 184mg Sodium. Exchanges: ½ Grain (Starch); 8½ Lean Meat; 0 Fat.

LC SERVING SUGGESTIONS: Mashed Faux-tay-toes (page 246) and sautéed green beans (see sidebar on page 251) should do it.

SERVING SUGGESTION: Add regular mashed potatoes.

# FRENCH ONION SOUP

1 tablespoon butter
1 tablespoon olive oil
3 onions, thinly sliced
Salt and pepper to taste
⅓ cup red wine (or red grape juice with a splash of vinegar)
1 tablespoon balsamic vinegar
2 cups beef broth
1 cup water
½ teaspoon thyme
⅓ cup croutons
½ cup shredded Swiss cheese

In a saucepan, heat together the butter and olive oil over medium-high heat. Add the onions and salt and pepper to taste, and turn the heat down to medium/medium-low. You want the onion to cook slowly and caramelize. This step takes a good 20 to 30 minutes (and can be done the night before). Make sure you stir it often so they won't stick and burn.

Add the wine, balsamic vinegar, beef broth, and water; bring to a boil. Add the thyme; taste and correct the seasoning by adding salt and pepper as necessary. Let simmer for about 15 minutes.

To finish, preheat the broiler. Divvy up the soup into 4 good-size, oven-proof and broiler-proof soup bowls and place them on a baking sheet. Now evenly distribute the croutons on top of the soup and sprinkle the Swiss cheese on top of that. Broil till cheese is bubbly and slightly browned. Serve immediately.

**PER SERVING**
195 Calories; 10g Fat (50.9% calories from fat); 11g Protein; 12g Carbohydrate; 2g Dietary Fiber; 21mg Cholesterol; 739mg Sodium. Exchanges: 0 Grain (Starch); 1 Lean Meat; 1 Vegetable; 0 Fruit; 1½ Fat.

**LC SERVING SUGGESTION:** Serve with a big spinach salad.

**SERVING SUGGESTION:** Add whole-grain rolls.

# SEARED SALMON WITH
# LEMON SAUCE

*Serves 4*

*Salt and pepper to taste*
*4 salmon fillets*
*1 tablespoon olive oil*
*¼ cup chicken broth*
*½ lemon, cut in wedges and with seeds removed*
*1 tablespoon butter*

Heat your skillet over medium-high heat for about 3 minutes or so (I prefer a stainless skillet for this rather than a nonstick). While the skillet is heating, salt and pepper your salmon on both sides.

Add the olive oil to the hot skillet and move it around to coat. Give it a minute to heat.

Add the salmon fillets and cook for about 3 minutes on each side. Remove them from the skillet and keep warm.

Add the chicken broth to the pan and, using a wire whisk, deglaze the pan well. Allow this mixture to reduce slightly. Now squeeze the lemon into the pan and whisk again. Take pan off the heat and whisk in the butter till well incorporated. Serve immediately with the sauce spooned over the top of the seared fish.

PER SERVING
256 Calories; 12g Fat (43.9% calories from fat); 34g Protein; 1g Carbohydrate; trace Dietary Fiber; 96mg Cholesterol; 191mg Sodium. Exchanges: 5 Lean Meat; 0 Fruit; 1 Fat.

LC SERVING SUGGESTIONS: Serve with steamed broccoli and Baked Cheesy Cauliflower (page 247).

SERVING SUGGESTION: Add steamed red potatoes.

# PEGGY'S SOUTHWEST CRUSTLESS QUICHE

*Serves 4*

*2 tablespoons wheat germ*
*1 cup cooked turkey breast, no skin, chopped*
*4 ounces green chili peppers, drained*
*1 cup onion, chopped fine*
*2 ounces Cheddar cheese, grated*
*2 ounces Swiss cheese, grated*
*5 eggs*
*½ cup half-and-half*
*½ cup salsa—your favorite*
*⅛ teaspoon nutmeg*
*Salt and pepper to taste*

Preheat oven to 375 degrees F.

Lightly grease a 9-inch pie pan. Add the wheat germ to the bottom of the pan and shake it around to distribute evenly on the bottom.

In a large mixing bowl, combine the turkey, chilies, onion, and cheeses. Place this mixture on the bottom of the pie plate.

In that same (now empty) bowl, add the eggs, half-and-half, salsa, nutmeg, and salt and pepper to taste. Mix well and pour this mixture carefully over the turkey mixture.

Bake in the oven for 30 to 40 minutes until the center is set and a knife inserted in the middle comes out clean. Let cool 10 minutes before slicing.

**PER SERVING**
305 Calories; 19g Fat (55.2% calories from fat); 27g Protein; 6g Carbohydrate; 1g Dietary Fiber; 300mg Cholesterol; 239mg Sodium. Exchanges: 0 Grain (Starch); 3½ Lean Meat; ½ Vegetable; 0 Non-Fat Milk; 2½ Fat.

**LC SERVING SUGGESTION:** Serve with a big green salad.

**SERVING SUGGESTION:** Add a bowl of baby carrots and cherry tomatoes.

# ASIAN PORK STIR-FRY

*1 pound boneless pork, cut into strips*

*½ small onion, peeled and cut lengthwise into thin slices*

*3 tablespoons low-sodium soy sauce*

*1 teaspoon sherry or water*

*2 teaspoons cornstarch*

*¼ teaspoon ground ginger*

*2 dashes black pepper*

*1 tablespoon olive oil, divided*

*12 ounces snow peas, rinsed and stringed*

*12 medium mushrooms, thinly sliced*

In a large, zipper-topped plastic bag, combine the pork, onion, soy sauce, sherry, cornstarch, ginger, and pepper and marinate for 10 to 15 minutes in the fridge while you finish preparing the rest of the meal.

In a wok or a skillet, heat half the oil over medium-high heat. Add the pork mixture and any remaining marinade to this and stir-fry till pork is nearly cooked through, about 5 minutes. Now add in the rest of the oil, snow peas, and mushrooms and finish cooking in the wok. The meal is finished when the mushrooms are tender.

**PER SERVING**
290 Calories; 12g Fat (37.1% calories from fat); 33g Protein; 12g Carbohydrate; 3g Dietary Fiber; 54mg Cholesterol; 1853mg Sodium. Exchanges: 0 Grain (Starch); 4 Lean Meat; 2 Vegetable; ½ Fat.

**LC SERVING SUGGESTION:** Serve on a bed of spaghetti squash.

**SERVING SUGGESTION:** Add brown rice.

# CROCK ROAST WITH
# A RED WINE SAUCE

*Serves 4*

*1 onion, sliced thin*
*4 cloves garlic, cut in half*
*1 tablespoon olive oil*
*1½ pounds chuck roast, fat removed*
*Salt and pepper to taste*
*1 teaspoon Dijon mustard*
*1 teaspoon brown sugar*
*¾ cup red wine (or red grape juice with a splash of vinegar)*
*¾ cup beef broth*
*1 bay leaf*

On the bottom of the Crock-Pot, lay the onion and garlic down. In a Dutch oven or skillet, heat the olive oil over medium-high heat. Brown the roast on all sides, and salt and pepper as you go. Add it to the Crock-Pot on top of the onion and garlic.

Now mix together the mustard, brown sugar, wine, and broth. Add this over the top of the roast and throw in the bay leaf.

Cook on low 8 hours, depending on the type of slow cooker you have. Remove roast from the Crock-Pot and pour juices into a saucepan (don't forget to remove the bay leaf) and heat over medium-high heat. When the sauce comes to a boil, lower the heat and let simmer. You want the sauce to reduce slightly. Taste for seasoning and, after slicing the roast, serve with cooking juices over the top.

PER SERVING
446 Calories; 30g Fat (65.8% calories from fat); 29g Protein; 6g Carbohydrate; 1g Dietary Fiber; 98mg Cholesterol; 371mg Sodium. Exchanges: 4 Lean Meat; ½ Vegetable; 3½ Fat; 0 Other Carbohydrates.

LC SERVING SUGGESTIONS: Serve with braised red cabbage (see sidebar on page 254) and steamed broccoli.

SERVING SUGGESTIONS: Add mashed potatoes.

# WINTER

# ❄ Week One

**DAY ONE:** Pepper-Stuffed Herb Chicken
**DAY TWO:** Pork Chops Diane
**DAY THREE:** Asian Salmon Patties
**DAY FOUR:** Mexican Flank Steak
**DAY FIVE:** Low-Carb Turkey Divan
**DAY SIX:** Crock Goulash

## SHOPPING LIST

### MEAT

4 chicken breasts (with skin and bone)
4 boneless loin pork chops (about 1 pound total)
1½ pounds boneless pork (cut into 1-inch cubes)
2 cups turkey breast cutlets
2 cups salmon (cooked, if not buying canned)
1 pound beef flank steak

### CONDIMENTS

olive oil
sesame oil
lime juice
vinegar (if not using white wine or sherry)
Worcestershire sauce
ketchup
Dijon mustard
**lc mayonnaise
**lc rice vinegar
**lc balsamic vinegar

**PRODUCE**

3 pounds onions (keep on hand)

1 bunch green onions

1 bunch cilantro; **lc additional

1 head garlic

1 piece gingerroot (you'll need 1 tablespoon)

2 red bell peppers

2 lemons (you'll need 2 tablespoons juice)

1 lime

1 head red cabbage (you'll need 2 cups shredded)

1 bunch parsley

**lc kale (1 meal)

**lc 2 bags spinach (2 meals)

**lc 1 bag coleslaw mix (1 meal)

**lc 1 bunch Swiss chard (1 meal)

**lc 1 head cauliflower (1 meal)

**lc rutabaga (1 meal)

**lc Hubbard squash (1 meal)

**lc 1 red onion (1 meal)

**russet potatoes (2 meals)

**CANNED GOODS**

1 14½-ounce can chicken broth

2 cups salmon, (if not buying fresh)

1 jar salsa (you'll need ½ cup)

**lc dry-roasted peanuts (crushed)

**SPICES**

oregano

basil

paprika
lemon pepper
crushed red pepper
**lc nutmeg

DAIRY/DAIRY CASE
butter
sour cream (you'll need ½ cup); **extra for garnish
Feta cheese (you'll need ¼ cup)
Romano cheese (you'll need ¼ cup grated)
1 egg
half-and-half (you'll need ¼ cup)
**lc 8-ounce package cream cheese
**milk

DRY GOODS
whole-wheat flour
**lc white sugar or Splenda
**lc walnuts
**1–2 pounds brown rice (2 meals)
**1 package angel hair pasta (1 meal)

FROZEN FOODS
1 10-ounce bag frozen broccoli flowerets

BAKERY
**whole-wheat hamburger buns
**whole-wheat-flour tortillas

OTHER
white wine (you'll need ¾ cup, if not using white grape
    juice)

sherry (you'll need 1 tablespoon, if not using red grape juice)

white grape juice (you'll need ¾ cup, if not using white wine)

red grape juice (you'll need 1 tablespoon, if not using sherry)

# PEPPER-STUFFED HERB CHICKEN

*Serves 4*

*1 tablespoon olive oil*
*1 onion, chopped*
*2 red bell peppers, cut into strips*
*2 cloves garlic, pressed*
*Salt and pepper to taste*
*½ teaspoon oregano*
*½ teaspoon basil*
*¼ cup Feta cheese*
*4 chicken breasts (with skin and bone)*
*¾ cup white wine (or white grape juice with a splash of vinegar)*
*1 tablespoon butter*

Preheat oven to 425 degrees F.

In a skillet, heat the olive oil, add the onion, pepper, garlic, salt and pepper, and herbs and cook till onion is translucent and peppers are soft. Let cool. When cooled, add the cheese, tossing well to distribute.

In the meantime, prepare chicken. Loosen the skin of the chicken and stuff ¼ of the mixture in between skin and flesh. Sprinkle the tops of the chicken with salt and pepper, and place in a metal baking dish.

Roast chicken for about 30 to 40 minutes or until chicken juices run clear when pierced with a fork. Remove the chicken from the pan and keep warm.

Heat the pan on the stovetop, about medium-high heat. Add the white wine and, using a wire whisk, get all the browned goodies up off the bottom of the pan, whisking as you go. Let the pan juices reduce to about half. Remove from heat, add the butter, whisk well, and serve over the top of the chicken.

**PER SERVING**
639 Calories; 35g Fat (52.9% calories from fat); 63g Protein; 8g Carbohydrate; 2g Dietary Fiber; 202mg Cholesterol; 321mg Sodium. Exchanges: 0 Grain (Starch); 9 Lean Meat; 1 Vegetable; 1½ Fat.

**LC SERVING SUGGESTIONS:** Serve with braised kale (see sidebar on page 254) and some baked Hubbard squash.

**SERVING SUGGESTION:** Add brown rice.

# PORK CHOPS DIANE

*Serves 4*

> 4 boneless loin pork chops (about a pound, total)
> 2 teaspoons lemon pepper
> 2 tablespoons butter
> 2 tablespoons lemon juice
> 1 tablespoon Worcestershire sauce
> 1 teaspoon Dijon mustard
> 1 tablespoon minced parsley

Sprinkle surfaces of chops with lemon pepper. Heat butter in heavy skillet over medium-high heat; cook chops for 3 to 4 minutes on each side, or until cooked through. Remove from skillet and keep warm.

To the skillet, add the lemon juice, Worcestershire sauce, and mustard. Cook, stirring up the browned bits with a wire whisk and mixing with pan juices, until heated through. Pour sauce over chops, sprinkle with parsley, and serve.

**PER SERVING**
191 Calories; 11g Total Fat (45% calories from fat); 25g Protein; 2g Dietary Fiber; 2g Carbohydrate; 71mg Cholesterol; 332mg Sodium. Exchanges: 0 Grain (Starch); 3½ Lean Meat; 0 Vegetable; 0 Fruit; 1 Fat; 0 Other Carbohydrates.

**LC SERVING SUGGESTIONS:** Serve with Sautéed Garlicky Spinach (page 253) and Mashed Rutabagas (page 249).

**SERVING SUGGESTION:** Add baked russet potatoes.

# ASIAN SALMON PATTIES

*Serves 4*

*2 cups salmon, canned (drained), or cooked and chopped*
*4 green onions, chopped*
*1 tablespoon gingerroot, grated*
*1 egg, lightly beaten*
*Salt and pepper to taste*
*¼ teaspoon crushed red pepper*
*½ teaspoon sesame oil*
*1 tablespoon olive oil*
*Chopped cilantro*
*1 lime, cut in fourths*

In a bowl, combine all ingredients except olive oil, chopped cilantro, and lime wedges.

Carefully form four patties, firmly packing the patties so they won't fall apart.

In a skillet, heat the olive oil over medium-high heat. Add the patties and brown, about 3 to 5 minutes on each side, turning only once. When you turn, be very careful or they can fall apart.

Serve with cilantro sprinkled over the top and a lime wedge on the side.

**PER SERVING**
199 Calories; 9g Fat (42.0% calories from fat); 25g Protein; 3g Carbohydrate; 1g Dietary Fiber; 108mg Cholesterol; 96mg Sodium. Exchanges: 0 Grain (Starch); 3½ Lean Meat; ½ Vegetable; 0 Fruit; 1 Fat.

**LC SERVING SUGGESTION**: Serve with Asian Slaw (page 255).

**SERVING SUGGESTION**: Add a whole-wheat hamburger bun and serve like a burger. You can add the cilantro to a little mayo to help hold everything together.

# MEXICAN FLANK STEAK

*Serves 4*

## LIVING LA VIDA LOCA

❋ When you love Mexican food and go low carb, saying adios to tortillas is hard to swallow. Thank heavens for La Tortilla Factory. La Tortilla Factory makes excellent low-carb tortillas. I mention them by name in this book for several reasons:

- They are trans-fat free. Most tortillas are loaded with shortening and/or hydrogenated oils of some sort.
- They are lard free. No explanation needed on why that's important.
- Their whole-wheat tortillas contain 9 grams of fiber per serving.
- They contain only 3 net carbs per tortilla.
- They are available nationwide in grocery stores, but if you can't get them at your store, you can order them on their website, www.latortillafactory.com.

These tortillas are definitely worth seeking out!

*¼ cup lime juice*
*2 tablespoons olive oil*
*½ cup salsa, divided*
*Salt and pepper to taste*
*1 pound beef flank steak*
*2 tablespoons fresh cilantro, chopped*

In a large, zipper-topped plastic bag, combine lime juice, olive oil, half the salsa, and salt and pepper. Place beef flank steak in plastic bag, turning to coat. Close bag securely and marinate in refrigerator at least 6 to 8 hours (overnight is ideal), turning occasionally.

Preheat broiler. Remove beef from the bag and discard marinade. Place beef in a broiler-proof baking pan (NOT glass) and broil 5 inches away from heat; cook about 5 to 7 minutes on each side for medium rare or cook to desired doneness.

Slice meat diagonally and serve with remaining salsa and cilantro sprinkled over the top.

### PER SERVING
297 Calories; 19g Fat (57.5% calories from fat); 23g Protein; 8g Carbohydrate; 2g Dietary Fiber; 58mg Cholesterol; 88mg Sodium. Exchanges: 0 Grain (Starch); 3 Lean Meat; 1 Vegetable; 0 Fruit; 2 Fat.

LC SERVING SUGGESTIONS: Serve with a spinach salad made with a little red onion and walnuts. Serve with Balsamic Vinaigrette (page 254).

SERVING SUGGESTION: Add some whole-wheat-flour tortillas and wrap up the meat for a tasty burrito.

# LOW-CARB TURKEY DIVAN

*Serves 4*

*¼ cup butter*

*⅛ cup whole-wheat flour*

*½ can chicken broth*

*¼ cup half-and-half*

*Salt and pepper to taste*

*1 tablespoon sherry (or red grape juice with a splash of vinegar)*

*1 10-ounce bag frozen broccoli flowerets, steamed*

*2 cups turkey breast cutlets, cooked and diced*

*¼ cup Romano cheese, grated*

Preheat oven to 350 degrees F.

In a saucepan, melt butter over medium-low heat. Add in the flour, using a wire whisk. Now add the chicken broth and half-and-half, stirring and whisking till slightly thickened, but do not boil or the sauce will break. Salt and pepper to taste, and add the sherry.

Place the broccoli in a 13- × 9-inch baking dish. Then add the turkey to the top of that. Pour sauce evenly over the top, sprinkle the cheese on top, and bake for about 20 minutes or until cheese starts to brown (but don't let it get too brown).

PER SERVING
310 Calories; 17g Fat (49.6% calories from fat); 31g Protein; 8g Carbohydrate; 3g Dietary Fiber; 110mg Cholesterol; 552mg Sodium. Exchanges: 0 Grain (Starch); 4 Lean Meat; 1 Vegetable; 0 Non-Fat Milk; 3 Fat.

LC SERVING SUGGESTIONS: Serve with Mashed Faux-tay-toes (page 246) and a big green salad.

SERVING SUGGESTION: Add mashed potatoes.

# CROCK GOULASH

*1 tablespoon olive oil*
*1½ pounds boneless pork, cut into 1-inch cubes*
*1 onion, halved and thinly sliced*
*Salt and pepper to taste*
*¼ cup water*
*3 tablespoons ketchup*
*1 tablespoon paprika*
*2 cloves garlic, pressed*
*2 cups shredded red cabbage*
*1 tablespoon whole-wheat flour*
*½ cup sour cream, plus extra for garnish*

In a skillet, heat the olive oil over medium-high heat. Brown the pork and onion together; salt and pepper as you go. In the Crock-Pot, combine pork, onion, water, ketchup, paprika, garlic, pepper, and cabbage. Cover and cook on low for 7 to 8 hours, depending on the type of slow cooker you have, or until pork is tender.

At the last hour of cooking, combine flour and sour cream. Stir into pork mixture and blend thoroughly. Keep the lid off the Crock-Pot and give it a stir now and then. Serve with a dollop of sour cream on top.

**PER SERVING**
305 Calories; 14g Fat (40.9% calories from fat); 33g Protein; 12g Carbohydrate; 2g Dietary Fiber; 90mg Cholesterol; 218mg Sodium. Exchanges: 0 Grain (Starch); 4½ Lean Meat; 1 Vegetable; 0 Non-Fat Milk; 1½ Fat; 0 Other Carbohydrates.

**LC SERVING SUGGESTION:** Serve on a bed of sautéed Swiss chard (see sidebar on page 251).

**SERVING SUGGESTION:** Serve with brown rice, too.

# ❄ **Week Two**

**DAY ONE:** Shrimp Scampi

**DAY TWO:** Skillet Chicken with Apple-Cider Sauce

**DAY THREE:** Classic Salisbury Steak and Mushrooms

**DAY FOUR:** Tuscan Pork Chops

**DAY FIVE:** Baked Salmon with Cilantro Pesto

**DAY SIX:** RECIPE RAVE: Caroline's Cheesy Crock Cauliflower Soup

## SHOPPING LIST

### MEAT

4 boneless, skinless chicken breast halves

1 pound extra-lean ground beef

4 boneless pork chops

1 pound large raw shrimp (peeled and deveined, if not buying frozen)

4 salmon fillets

4 slices turkey bacon

### CONDIMENTS

olive oil

vinegar (if not using white or red wine)

**lc salad dressing—your favorite

### PRODUCE

3 pounds onions (keep on hand)

2 heads garlic (you'll need 9 cloves)

2 tomatoes; **lc 1 extra

mushrooms (you'll need 3 cups sliced)

1 medium stalk celery

1 medium carrot

1 lemon

1 lime (you'll need 1 tablespoon juice)

1 apple

1 bunch parsley (you'll need ¼ cup chopped)

1 bunch cilantro (you'll need 1¼ cups)

**lc 3 heads lettuce (*not* iceberg) (3 meals)

**lc salad vegetables (2 meals)

**lc kale (1 meal)

**lc bok choy (1 meal)

**lc 1 head broccoli (1 meal)

**lc 1 head cauliflower (1 meal)

**lc spaghetti squash (1 meal)

**lc pumpkin wedges (1 meal)

**lc 1 avocado (1 meal)

**lc snow-pea pods (1meal)

**lc green beans (1 meal)

**lc turnips (1 meal)

**lc 1 red onion

**russet potatoes (1 meal)

**red potatoes (1 meal)

## CANNED GOODS

apple cider (you'll need ½ cup)

2 14½-ounce cans chicken broth

1 14½-ounce can beef broth

## SPICES

thyme

rosemary

## DAIRY/DAIRY CASE

butter

1 egg

milk

low-fat Cheddar cheese (you'll need 1½ cups)

**lc 8-ounce package cream cheese (1 meal)

**lc Romano cheese (garnish)

### DRY GOODS

cornstarch

pine nuts (you'll need ½ cup)

**1 pound brown rice (1 meal)

### FROZEN FOODS

1 pound large raw shrimp (peeled and deveined, if not
buying fresh)

2 8-ounce packages frozen cauliflower

### BAKERY

1 package low-carb whole-wheat bread (you'll need 2
tablespoons crumbs)

**whole-wheat rolls

### OTHER

white wine (you'll need ¼ cup, if not using white grape
juice)

red wine (you'll need ¼ cup, if not using red grape juice)

white grape juice (you'll need ¼ cup, if not using white
wine)

red grape juice (you'll need ¼ cup, if not using red wine)

# SHRIMP SCAMPI

*Serves 4*

1 tablespoon butter
1 tablespoon olive oil
3 cloves garlic, pressed
1 pound large raw shrimp, peeled and deveined
1 tomato, diced
¼ cup white wine (or white grape juice with a splash of vinegar)
Juice of 1 lemon
Salt and pepper to taste
¼ cup parsley, finely chopped

In a skillet, heat butter and olive oil together over medium-high heat. Add the garlic, sauté for 1 minute, then add the shrimp and tomato. Sauté for 1 minute, add wine, lemon juice, and salt and pepper to taste. The sauce will reduce and shrimp will turn pink—it happens very quickly. Do not overcook or the shrimp will be rubbery. Sprinkle with parsley before serving.

**PER SERVING**
190 Calories; 8g Fat (42.2% calories from fat); 23g Protein; 2g Carbohydrate; 2g Dietary Fiber; 180mg Cholesterol; 200mg Sodium. Exchanges: 3 Lean Meat; 0 Vegetable; 1 Fat.

**LC SERVING SUGGESTIONS:** Serve on a bed of spaghetti squash. Grate some Romano cheese over the top. Add some sautéed green beans (see sidebar on page 251) for a wonderful meal.

**SERVING SUGGESTION:** Instead of the spaghetti squash, serve on a bed of angel hair pasta.

# SKILLET CHICKEN WITH APPLE-CIDER SAUCE

*Serves 4*

1 tablespoon olive oil
4 boneless, skinless chicken breast halves
Salt and pepper to taste
½ onion, chopped
4 turkey bacon slices, diced
½ apple, diced
1 teaspoon thyme
¼ cup chicken broth
½ cup apple cider
1 tablespoon butter

In a skillet, heat the olive oil. Add the chicken, and salt and pepper to taste. Brown the chicken on both sides, about 5 minutes each side. Remove chicken and keep warm.

Add the onion and turkey bacon to the skillet. Cook till onion is translucent and bacon has browned a bit, about 5 minutes. Now add the apple and thyme, and salt and pepper again to taste. When apples are browned and soft, add the broth and cider. Turn the heat up and, with a wire whisk, cook the sauce till it thickens up, stirring frequently. Add the butter and whisk till melted in. Return the chicken back to the skillet for about 2 minutes, thoroughly coating in sauce. Serve with more sauce on the top of the chicken.

**PER SERVING**
253 Calories; 11g Fat (38.7% calories from fat); 30g Protein; 8g Carbohydrate; 1g Dietary Fiber; 89mg Cholesterol; 339mg Sodium. Exchanges: 0 Grain (Starch); 4 Lean Meat; 0 Vegetable; ½ Fruit; 1½ Fat.

LC SERVING SUGGESTIONS: Serve with braised kale (see sidebar on page 254) and garlicky turnips (page 129).

SERVING SUGGESTION: Add brown rice.

## NO CHICKENING OUT

❋ Nearly every week, the shopping lists will contain boneless, skinless chicken breast halves. These are the kind you can buy frozen, individually flash frozen, and in large 3-pound bags. I suggest you use the frozen ones (as opposed to the fresh) for several reasons. One, they're usually less expensive this way. Very often markets will have them on sale—buy one/get one free. Two, the frozen factor is helpful for recipes that need the chicken cut in strips, cubes, and so forth. Semifrozen chicken is much easier to cut than fresh, wiggly chicken.

# CLASSIC SALISBURY STEAK AND MUSHROOMS

*Serves 4*

*1 pound extra-lean ground beef*
*2 tablespoons whole-wheat bread crumbs*
*Salt and pepper to taste*
*1 teaspoon thyme*
*1 egg*
*1 onion, sliced and separated into rings*
*3 cups sliced mushrooms*
*1 14½-ounce can beef broth*
*2 tablespoons cold water*
*2 teaspoons cornstarch*

In a mixing bowl, mix together the ground beef, bread crumbs, salt and pepper, thyme, and egg. Shape into 4 nice-size patties, about ¾ of an inch thick.

In a skillet over medium heat, cook the beef patties, turning when necessary, until browned, about 10 minutes. Remove patties to a plate lined with paper towels to absorb the fat. Add the onion and mushrooms to the skillet and sauté till nicely browned. Add the broth to the skillet, heat to boiling, and reduce the heat. Add the patties back to the skillet, cover; simmering till patties are thoroughly cooked, about 10 minutes.

Now remove the patties again and keep warm. In a small bowl, mix together the cold water and cornstarch till smooth (no lumps allowed). Whisk into the skillet and turn up the heat, whisking as you go. The sauce will thicken; serve it over the patties.

**PER SERVING**
339 Calories; 21g Fat (56.1% calories from fat); 27g Protein; 10g Carbohydrate; 2g Dietary Fiber; 125mg Cholesterol; 440mg Sodium. Exchanges: ½ Grain (Starch); 3½ Lean Meat; 1 Vegetable; 2 Fat.

**LC SERVING SUGGESTIONS:** Serve with Mashed Faux-tay-toes (page 246), Baked Pumpkin Wedges (page 252), and a big green salad.

**SERVING SUGGESTION:** Add mashed potatoes.

# TUSCAN PORK CHOPS

*Serves 4*

*1 tablespoon olive oil*
*4 boneless pork chops*
*Salt and pepper to taste*
*4 cloves garlic, pressed*
*1 teaspoon rosemary, crushed*
*1 tomato, diced*
*¼ cup red wine (or use red grape juice with a splash of vinegar)*
*½ cup chicken broth*
*1 tablespoon butter*

In a skillet, heat the olive oil over medium-high heat. Add the chops, and salt and pepper to taste. Brown on both sides, about 5 minutes per side, depending on how thick they are. Remove the chops and keep warm.

To the skillet, add the garlic, rosemary, tomato, red wine, and chicken broth. Turn up the heat and cook sauce; using a wire whisk, whisk up the browned bits off the bottom of the pan. Let sauce reduce and remove from the heat. Add the butter. When it is melted and incorporated into the sauce, add the chops back in and thoroughly coat. Then remove chops to dinner plates; serve with sauce ladled over the top.

**PER SERVING**
218 Calories; 11g Fat (51.9% calories from fat); 21g Protein; 3g Carbohydrate; 1g Dietary Fiber; 59mg Cholesterol; 76mg Sodium. Exchanges: 0 Grain (Starch); 3 Lean Meat; ½ Vegetable; 1½ Fat.

**LC SERVING SUGGESTIONS:** Serve with sautéed snow peas and a green salad.

**SERVING SUGGESTION:** Add red potatoes.

# BAKED SALMON WITH CILANTRO PESTO

*Serves 4*

*4 salmon fillets*
*Salt and pepper to taste*

### CILANTRO PESTO

*1 ¼ cups cilantro*
*1 tablespoon lime juice*
*2 tablespoons olive oil*
*2 cloves garlic, pressed*
*Salt and pepper to taste*
*½ cup pine nuts*

Preheat oven to 400 degrees F.

Lightly grease an 8-inch-square baking dish. Place the fillets in the dish, and salt and pepper to taste. Cook for about 10 to 20 minutes, depending on how thick the fish is, or until fish flakes easily with a fork.

To make the Cilantro Pesto: In a blender, add the rest of the ingredients and blend till smooth (add a little water or more olive oil if too thick). Serve ladled onto the salmon.

### PER SERVING

382 Calories; 22g Fat (50.4% calories from fat); 40g Protein; 8g Carbohydrate; 2g Dietary Fiber; 88mg Cholesterol; 134mg Sodium. Exchanges: ½ Grain (Starch); 5½ Lean Meat; 0 Vegetable; 0 Fruit; 2½ Fat.

LC SERVING SUGGESTIONS: Serve with braised bok choy (see sidebar on page 254) and steamed broccoli.

SERVING SUGGESTION: Add brown rice.

## ✳ Recipe Rave:
## CAROLINE'S CHEESY CROCK CAULIFLOWER SOUP

*Serves 4*

"We just love Caroline's Cheesy Crock Cauliflower Soup. It is definitely a *rave* in our household!"

—LOTTIE

2 cups chicken broth
2 8-ounce packages frozen cauliflower
1 medium stalk celery, chopped
1 medium carrot, chopped
1 small onion, chopped
½ teaspoon thyme
Salt and pepper to taste
1 cup milk
1½ cup shredded low-fat Cheddar cheese

Throw all ingredients except milk and cheese into a Crock-Pot and cook on low until vegetables are very tender, about 4 to 6 hours, depending on the type of slow cooker you have.

Carefully pour mixture into work bowl of food processor fitted with a steel blade or into blender container. Cover and process until smooth. Or, if you like it a little lumpy and bumpy like I do, use a potato masher and have at it in the Crock-Pot itself; mash to your heart's delight.

Place your cauliflower mixture into a saucepan; stir in milk and cheese. Heat over medium heat, stirring constantly, until cheese is melted and mixture is hot.

PER SERVING
235 Calories; 16g Total Fat (59% calories from fat); 15g Protein; 8g Carbohydrate; 1g Dietary Fiber; 46mg Cholesterol; 701mg Sodium. Exchanges: 0 Grain (Starch); 1½ Lean Meat; 1 Vegetable; 0 Fruit; 2 Fat; 0 Other Carbohydrates.

LC SERVING SUGGESTIONS: A huge, hearty salad (add sliced avocado, tomatoes, and red onion to your choice of lettuce(s)/greens).

SERVING SUGGESTION: Add warmed whole-wheat rolls to above.

## ❄ Week Three

**DAY ONE:** Roast Brazilian Chicken

**DAY TWO:** Nutty Oven-Fried Fish

**DAY THREE:** Winter Sausage Soup

**DAY FOUR:** Pork Piccata

**DAY FIVE:** Garlicky Seared Scallops on Greens

**DAY SIX:** Southwestern Crock Beef Stew

### SHOPPING LIST

#### MEAT

4 chicken breasts (with skin and bone)

4 boneless pork chops (about ½ inch thick)

4 fish fillets

1 pound scallops

1 pound boneless top round

12 ounces turkey kielbasa

#### CONDIMENTS

balsamic vinegar

olive oil

vegetable oil

**lc salad dressing—your choice

**lc prepared low-carb tartar sauce (if not making your own)

**lc mayonnaise (2 meals)

#### PRODUCE

3 pounds onions (keep on hand)

1 head garlic (7 cloves)

2 turnips

celery (you'll need 1 stalk)

1 carrot

3–5 lemons (you'll need 2 lemons + 2 tablespoons juice)

1 bunch kale

2 bags spinach (you'll need 6 cups)

2 medium zucchini

1 large red bell pepper

1 bunch cilantro—optional, for topping

**lc 3 heads lettuce (*not* iceberg) (3 meals)

**lc 1 bag coleslaw mix (1 meal)

**lc 1 head red cabbage (1 meal)

**lc green onions (for homemade tartar sauce)

**lc turnips (1 meal)

**lc 3 heads broccoli (3 meals)

**lc 1 head cauliflower (1 meal)

**rutabagas (2 meals)

**lc Hubbard squash (1 meal)

**lc salad vegetables (3 meals)

**russet potatoes (2 meals)

### CANNED GOODS

4 14½-ounce cans chicken broth (3 cans + ⅓ cup)

1 14½-ounce can beef broth

1 jar salsa (you'll need ¾ cup)

capers (you'll need 1 tablespoon); **lc extra for homemade tartar sauce

**lc dill pickles (for homemade tartar sauce)

### SPICES

paprika

oregano

cumin

thyme

crushed red pepper

**garlic powder

**DAIRY/DAIRY CASE**

butter

buttermilk (you'll need ½ cup)

Romano cheese (you'll need 1 tablespoon)

sour cream—optional; **extra for garnish

**DRY GOODS**

seasoned bread crumbs (you'll need ⅓ cup)

whole-wheat flour

cornstarch

almonds (¼ cup crushed)

**3 pounds brown rice (3 meals)

**BAKERY**

**whole-grain rolls (1 meal)

# ROAST BRAZILIAN CHICKEN

*Serves 4*

*4 chicken breasts (with skin and bone)*
*1 tablespoon balsamic vinegar*
*1 tablespoon olive oil*
*2 cloves garlic, pressed*
*1 teaspoon paprika*
*½ teaspoon oregano*
*½ teaspoon cumin*
*Salt and pepper to taste*

In a big zipper-topped plastic bag, add all ingredients and mush around to get the chicken and marinade well incorporated.

Refrigerate for at least 2 hours, preferably overnight. Turn the bag as often as you remember, to get the flavors distributed.

Preheat the oven to 500 degrees F.

Place the chicken in a metal baking pan, skin side down, and dispose of remaining marinade. Cook chicken for 10 minutes, then turn the chicken over and cook another 10 minutes. Chicken should be done through, but may require a little extra time depending on the size of the chicken breast.

PER SERVING
535 Calories; 30g Fat (52.4% calories from fat); 61g Protein; 1g Carbohydrate; trace Dietary Fiber; 186mg Cholesterol; 184mg Sodium. Exchanges: 0 Grain (Starch); 8½ Lean Meat; 0 Vegetable; 0 Fruit; ½ Fat.

LC SERVING SUGGESTIONS: Serve with Oven-Roasted Turnips (page 248), baked Hubbard squash, and a big green salad.

SERVING SUGGESTION: Add brown rice.

# NUTTY OVEN-FRIED FISH

*Serves 4*

*⅓ cup seasoned bread crumbs*
*¼ cup almonds, crushed*
*½ cup buttermilk*
*4 fish fillets*
*1 lemon, cut in quarters*

Preheat oven to 400 degrees F.

In a blender or a food processor, process together the bread crumbs and almonds till fine. Pour onto a dinner plate.

Pour the buttermilk into a bowl and dip in the fish fillets, one at a time. Then press the fish into the bread-crumb mixture.

Place the coated fish in a lightly greased baking pan. Cook fish for about 10 minutes or until fish flakes when tested with a fork. Serve with a lemon wedge.

**PER SERVING**
294 Calories; 7g Fat (20.9% calories from fat); 46g Protein; 12g Carbohydrate; 2g Dietary Fiber; 101mg Cholesterol; 423mg Sodium. Exchanges: ½ Grain (Starch); 5½ Lean Meat; 0 Fruit; 0 Non-Fat Milk; 1 Fat.

**LC SERVING SUGGESTIONS:** Serve fish with low-carb tartar sauce (to make, mix together mayo, capers, dill pickles, and green onions) Rutabaga Fries (page 249), and Basic Coleslaw (page 255).

**SERVING SUGGESTION:** Serve with Real Oven Fries (page 249).

# WINTER SAUSAGE SOUP

*Serves 4*

1 tablespoon olive oil

1 onion, chopped

3 cloves garlic, pressed

1 bunch kale, deveined and sliced in ribbons

2 turnips, peeled and chopped

1 stalk celery, chopped

1 carrot, chopped

½ teaspoon thyme

¼ teaspoon crushed red pepper

Salt and pepper to taste

3 cans chicken broth

12 ounces turkey kielbasa, sliced

1 tablespoon Romano cheese, grated

In a large saucepan, heat olive oil over medium-high heat. Add the onion and garlic and cook for a minute until fragrant. Now add the kale and keep sautéing about 2 more minutes. Add the turnips, celery, and carrot, cook 1 more minute. Add the spices, salt and pepper to taste, and all the chicken broth. Bring to a simmer and cook till all is tender, about 10 minutes or so, depending on how big the veggies pieces are. (At this point, you can finish the soup and add the kielbasa and be done with it. Or, if you like your soup nice and thick, take half the soup and give it whirr in the blender, pour it back into the pot, stir it around, and proceed to the next paragraph. Just remember: If you do this step, no kielbasa in the blender. Ewww.)

Finally, add the kielbasa and simmer another 5 minutes. Serve with a little grated Romano cheese on the top.

PER SERVING
378 Calories; 28g Fat (67.4% calories from fat); 17g Protein; 13g Carbohydrate; 3g Dietary Fiber; 59mg Cholesterol; 1573mg Sodium. Exchanges: 0 Grain (Starch); 2 Lean Meat; 2 Vegetable; 4 Fat.

LC SERVING SUGGESTION: A big green salad.

SERVING SUGGESTION: Add some whole-grain rolls.

# PORK PICCATA

*4 boneless pork chops (about ½ inch thick)*
*2 tablespoons butter, divided*
*1 tablespoon olive oil*
*Salt and pepper to taste*
*2 tablespoons whole-wheat flour*
*⅓ cup chicken broth*
*Juice from 1 large lemon*
*1 tablespoon capers*

Place the pork chops, 2 at a time, in a large zipper-topped plastic bag. Using the bottom of a skillet, flatten the chops to about ¼ inch. You can use a rolling pin for this task instead, if you prefer.

In a skillet, melt half the butter and olive oil together over medium-high heat. Salt and pepper the pork on both sides. Dredge the pork in the flour.

Sauté the pork on each side at least 4 to 5 minutes, or until nicely browned. Remove the pork from the pan and keep warm.

To the skillet add the chicken broth and whisk up the browned bits off the bottom of the pan, cooking for about a minute. Now add the lemon juice and cook for another 1 or 2 minutes or until slightly reduced. Add the capers and remaining butter, and return the pork to the skillet, turning to coat. Serve with sauce spooned over the top.

PER SERVING
251 Calories; 16g Fat (57.1% calories from fat); 23g Protein; 4g Carbohydrate; 1g Dietary Fiber; 82mg Cholesterol; 194mg Sodium. Exchanges: 0 Grain (Starch); 3 Lean Meat; 0 Fruit; 2 Fat; 0 Other Carbohydrates.

LC SERVING SUGGESTIONS: Serve with steamed broccoli and braised red cabbage (see sidebar on page 254).

SERVING SUGGESTION: Add brown rice.

# GARLICKY SEARED
# SCALLOPS ON GREENS

*Serves 4*

*2 tablespoons lemon juice*
*3 tablespoons olive oil, divided*
*2 cloves garlic, pressed*
*1 tablespoon water*
*1 pound scallops*
*Salt and pepper to taste*
*6 cups spinach*

In a small bowl, whisk together lemon juice, half the olive oil, garlic, and the water. This is the dressing.

Heat the rest of the oil in a skillet over medium-high heat. Add the scallops and cook about 2 to 3 minutes on each side, depending on how big your scallops are. Don't overcook. Salt and pepper them to taste when cooked.

Using half the dressing you just made, toss the spinach. Now, evenly distribute the spinach among 4 plates, top with the cooked scallops, and then drizzle remaining dressing over the top.

PER SERVING
203 Calories; 11g Fat (49.2% calories from fat); 20g Protein; 5g Carbohydrate; 1g Dietary Fiber; 37mg Cholesterol; 219mg Sodium. Exchanges: 2½ Lean Meat; ½ Vegetable; 0 Fruit; 2 Fat.

LC SERVING SUGGESTIONS: Rutabaga Fries (page 249) and some steamed broccoli.

SERVING SUGGESTION: Add baked potatoes.

# SOUTHWESTERN CROCK
# BEEF STEW

*Serves 4*

*1 tablespoon vegetable oil*
*1 pound boneless top round, cut into 2-inch cubes*
*Salt and pepper to taste*
*1 can beef broth*
*¾ cup salsa*
*1 large red bell pepper, cut into 1-inch pieces*
*1½ teaspoons ground cumin*
*2 medium zucchini, cut in half lengthwise and sliced crosswise so*
  *¾ inch thick*
*2 tablespoons cornstarch*
*¼ cup water*

*Sour cream*
*Chopped fresh cilantro*

In a skillet, heat oil over medium-high heat until hot. Add beef (½ at a time) and stir-fry 2 minutes or until outside surface is no longer pink. (Do not overcook.) Remove from pan; season with salt and pepper to taste. Set aside.

In the same pan, combine the broth, salsa, bell pepper, and cumin. Bring to a boil; reduce heat to medium-low for just a minute. Now add all of this to the Crock-Pot. Add in raw zucchini as well.

Cook till beef is fork tender, about 7 hours on low, depending on the type of slow cooker you have. Dissolve cornstarch in ¼ cup of water and add mixture during the last hour; keep the lid off the Crock-Pot to help it thicken, otherwise, place it all in a large saucepan, and cook over medium-low heat till thickened up a bit.

Serve with a dollop of sour cream and a sprinkle of fresh cilantro, if you like.

PER SERVING
322 Calories; 20g Total Fat (56% calories from fat); 23g Protein; 2g Dietary Fiber; 12g Carbohydrate; 72mg Cholesterol; 747mg Sodium. Exchanges: ½ Grain (Starch); 3 Lean Meat; 1½ Vegetable; 0 Fruit; 2 Fat; 0 Other Carbohydrates.

**LC SERVING SUGGESTIONS:** Serve with steamed broccoli and cauliflower and a big green salad.

**SERVING SUGGESTION:** Add brown rice.

## ❄ Week Four

DAY ONE: Skillet Curry-Lime Chicken

DAY TWO: Sautéed Pan Fish with Warm Avocado Salsa

DAY THREE: Roast Garlic Pork Chops

DAY FOUR: Bang-Bang Taco Soup

DAY FIVE: Turkey Artichoke Casserole

DAY SIX: Crock Mock Beef Bourguignon

## SHOPPING LIST

### MEAT

4 boneless, skinless chicken breast halves

8 turkey breast cutlets

1 pound extra-lean ground beef

2 pounds top round steak

4 boneless pork sirloin chops, ½ inch thick

1½ pounds fish fillets

4 pieces turkey bacon

### CONDIMENTS

olive oil

vinegar

balsamic vinegar

**lc salad dressing—your choice

### PRODUCE

3 pounds onions (keep on hand)

1 small red onion

2 heads garlic (you'll need 15 cloves)

1 tomato

1 avocado

mushrooms (you'll need 1 cup sliced)

2 limes (1 lime + 1 tablespoon juice)

1 bunch cilantro (¾ cup + garnish)

**lc 3 heads lettuce (*not* iceberg) (3 meals)

**lc 1 bag spinach (1 meal)

**1 head red cabbage (1 meal)

**lc 2 heads broccoli (2 meals)

**lc 1 head cauliflower (1 meal)

**lc Brussels sprouts (1meal)

**lc green beans (2 meals)

**lc portobello mushrooms (1 meal)

**lc salad vegetables (3 meals)

**lc pumpkin (1 meal)

**red potatoes (1 meal)

**russet potatoes (2 meals)

### CANNED GOODS

4 14½-ounce cans chicken broth

1 14½-ounce can beef broth

1 jar salsa (you'll need ½ cup)

4-ounce jar marinated artichoke hearts

### SPICES

curry powder

rosemary

thyme

marjoram

**nutmeg

### DAIRY/DAIRY CASE

butter

low-fat Cheddar cheese (you'll need 1 cup); **lc 1⅓ cups
   extra for quesadillas

**lc 8-ounce package cream cheese

**sour cream (garnish)

**DRY GOODS**

whole-wheat flour

1 package taco seasoning mix

**2 pounds brown rice

**FROZEN FOODS**

**frozen corn (you'll need 1 cup), optional

**BAKERY**

**lc low-carb tortillas

**whole-wheat tortillas

**OTHER**

red wine (you'll need ½ cup, if not using red grape juice)

white wine (you'll need ½ cup, if not using white grape
    juice)

red grape juice (you'll need ½ cup, if not using red wine)

white grape juice (you'll need ½ cup, if not using white
    wine)

# SKILLET CURRY-LIME CHICKEN

*Serves 4*

*4 boneless, skinless chicken breast halves*
*1 tablespoon balsamic vinegar*
*Salt and pepper to taste*
*1 tablespoon curry powder*
*2 tablespoons whole-wheat flour*
*2 tablespoons olive oil*
*½ cup chicken broth*
*Juice from 1 lime*
*1 tablespoon butter*
*½ cup cilantro, chopped*

Rub the chicken with the balsamic vinegar. Then sprinkle one side with salt and pepper and half of the curry powder. Now sprinkle half of the flour on the chicken.

In a skillet, heat the olive oil over medium-high heat. Add the chicken, floured side down. Add the remaining curry and flour to the chicken in the pan carefully. Lower the heat to medium. You will want to cook breasts about 5 minutes on each side, depending on how thick the chicken is. (Hint: You can use a rolling pin to thin the partially thawed chicken. Be sure to use wax paper or plastic wrap between the chicken and the rolling pin, though. This is really easy to do when the chicken is still partly frozen.)

When chicken is cooked, remove from pan and keep warm. Add chicken broth and, using a wire whisk, whisk up the browned bits off the bottom of the pan. When sauce has reduced slightly, add the lime juice. Allow to cook another minute, then add the butter and cilantro. Once butter has melted and is incorporated into the sauce, it is ready. Pour over the top of the chicken and serve.

PER SERVING
214 Calories; 10g Fat (38.1% calories from fat); 28g Protein; 6g Carbohydrate; 2g Dietary Fiber; 78mg Cholesterol; 79mg Sodium. Exchanges: ½ Grain (Starch); 4 Lean Meat; 0 Fruit; 1½ Fat.

**LC SERVING SUGGESTIONS:** Sautéed green beans (see sidebar on page 251) and a big green salad. (Watch the carb count on your salad dressings. Dressings higher in fat usually have lower carb counts.)

**SERVING SUGGESTION:** Add steamed red potatoes.

# SAUTÉED PAN FISH WITH WARM AVOCADO SALSA

*Serves 4*

*1 tablespoon olive oil*
*1½ pounds fish fillets*
*Salt and pepper to taste*
*1 avocado, peeled and diced*
*1 small red onion, chopped*
*1 tomato, chopped*
*¼ cup cilantro, chopped*
*1 tablespoon lime juice*
*¼ cup chicken broth*

In a skillet, heat the olive oil over medium-high heat. Add the fish to the skillet and brown well on both sides. Salt and pepper the fillets to taste.

Meanwhile, place the avocado, onion, tomato, cilantro, and lime juice together in a small bowl. Gently toss to mix.

When fish is done cooking, remove from the skillet and keep warm.

Add the chicken broth to the skillet and, using a whisk, get everything up off the bottom of the pan. Carefully add the avocado mixture and toss quickly to coat. Place this on top of the fish and serve.

**PER SERVING**
280 Calories; 13g Fat (39.8% calories from fat); 33g Protein; 10g Carbohydrate; 3g Dietary Fiber; 73mg Cholesterol; 152mg Sodium. Exchanges: 0 Grain (Starch); 4 Lean Meat; 1 Vegetable; 0 Fruit; 2 Fat.

**LC SERVING SUGGESTIONS:** Serve with steamed broccoli and Pumpkin Puree (page 253).

**SERVING SUGGESTION:** Add brown rice.

# ROAST GARLIC PORK CHOPS

*Serves 4*

*4 boneless pork sirloin chops, ½ inch thick*
*8 cloves garlic, slivered*
*Salt and pepper to taste*
*1 teaspoon rosemary, crushed*
*¼ cup chicken broth*
*½ cup white wine (or white grape juice with a splash of vinegar)*
*1 tablespoon butter*

Preheat oven to 500 degrees F.

With the pointed end of a knife, make 4 slits on the top of each pork chop. Insert the garlic slivers into the slits. Salt and pepper the chops to taste, and crush the rosemary on top and try and get it into the slits as best you can.

Place chops into a metal baking pan. Roast for 10 minutes, then pull from the oven and carefully turn chops over.

Finish roasting another 10 minutes or until chops are completely cooked through. Remove chops from pan and keep warm. Add the chicken broth and white wine to the pan and place the pan on the stovetop over medium-high heat. Using a wire whisk, whisk up the goodies off the bottom of the pan and allow the sauce to reduce slightly. Whisk in the butter and when melted and fully incorporated, serve atop the chops.

PER SERVING
209 Calories; 10g Fat (46.7% calories from fat); 22g Protein; 2g Carbohydrate; trace Dietary Fiber; 74mg Cholesterol; 132mg Sodium. Exchanges: 0 Grain (Starch); 3 Lean Meat; ½ Vegetable; ½ Fat.

LC SERVING SUGGESTIONS: Braised red cabbage (see sidebar on page 254) and steamed Brussels sprouts.

SERVING SUGGESTION: Add a baked potato.

# BANG-BANG TACO SOUP

*Serves 4*

This is one of the fastest recipes I have ever devised, and, naturally, it was born out of a great need just to get dinner on the table. Little did I know it would be a huge hit! And while you can do all kinds of things to this soup to give it more veggies, and so on, the best part about it is that it's *so fast*. That's why it's called Bang-Bang Taco Soup. Bada bing, bada bang, it's done!

1 pound extra-lean ground beef
½ onion, chopped
1 package taco seasoning mix (or 2 tablespoons of my homemade
    taco seasoning blend; see sidebar on page 9)
½ cup salsa
2 14½-ounce cans chicken broth
1 cup shredded low-fat Cheddar cheese
Sour cream for garnish

In a saucepan, cook the ground beef with the onion till done through. Drain what little fat is left and blot with paper toweling.

Add the taco seasoning mix, salsa, and chicken broth. Cook till heated through. Ladle soup into 4 bowls and serve with ¼ cup cheese and a dollop of sour cream on top of each bowl.

PER SERVING
373 Calories; 22g Fat (54.8% calories from fat); 32g Protein; 9g Carbohydrate; 1g Dietary Fiber; 84mg Cholesterol; 1353mg Sodium. Exchanges: 4½ Lean Meat; ½ Vegetable; 2 Fat; ½ Other Carbohydrates.

LC SERVING SUGGESTIONS: Serve with Spinach Quesadillas (page 255) (using low-carb tortillas, of course) and a green salad.

SERVING SUGGESTIONS: Use whole-wheat tortillas instead of the low-carb ones. You could throw a cup of frozen corn in your soup, too.

# TURKEY ARTICHOKE CASSEROLE

*Serves 4*

*3 tablespoons butter, divided*
*1 tablespoon olive oil*
*8 turkey breast cutlets, cut in 1-inch strips*
*2 cloves garlic, pressed*
*1 cup mushrooms, sliced*
*1 4-ounce jar marinated artichoke hearts, drained*
*2 tablespoons whole-wheat flour*
*1 14½-ounce can chicken broth*

Preheat oven to 350 degrees F.

In a skillet over medium heat, add 1 tablespoon of the butter and the olive oil. Throw the turkey in to brown, then add the garlic and mushrooms and keep cooking till everything is smelling very delicious.

Transfer the turkey to a baking dish and arrange the artichoke hearts on top.

In the skillet, melt the remaining butter and add the flour, whisking to blend (no lumps!). Add broth and cook until nicely thickened, then pour over turkey mixture.

Bake the casserole, uncovered, at 350 degrees F for about 30 to 45 minutes.

**PER SERVING**
301 Calories; 15g Fat (44.7% calories from fat); 37g Protein; 5g Carbohydrate; 1g Dietary Fiber; 113mg Cholesterol; 621mg Sodium. Exchanges: 0 Grain (Starch); 5 Lean Meat; ½ Vegetable; 2½ Fat.

**LC SERVING SUGGESTIONS:** Steamed broccoli and a big green salad. (Watch the carb count on your salad dressings. Dressings higher in fat usually have lower carb counts.)

**SERVING SUGGESTION:** Add brown rice.

# CROCK MOCK BEEF BOURGUIGNON

*Serves 4*

*1 tablespoon olive oil*

*Salt and pepper to taste*

*2 pounds top round steak*

*4 pieces turkey bacon, cut in half*

*1 onion, chopped coarse*

*4 cloves garlic, pressed*

*1 teaspoon thyme*

*1 teaspoon marjoram*

*½ teaspoon rosemary*

*½ cup red wine (or red grape juice with a splash of vinegar)*

*½ cup beef broth*

In a skillet, heat the olive oil over medium-high heat. Salt and pepper the roast and brown on all sides in the hot oil.

Place the beef in the bottom of the Crock-Pot. Now add the turkey bacon to the skillet along with the onion and garlic; cook for about 2 minutes.

Throw this on top of the beef and add the rest of the ingredients. Cook on low for about 8 to 10 hours, depending on the type of slow cooker you have.

Slice, and serve with pot juices.

**PER SERVING**
501 Calories; 27g Fat (51.7% calories from fat); 52g Protein; 5g Carbohydrate; 1g Dietary Fiber; 119mg Cholesterol; 476mg Sodium. Exchanges: 0 Grain (Starch); 7 Lean Meat; ½ Vegetable; 1 Fat.

**LC SERVING SUGGESTIONS:** Serve with Mashed Faux-tay-toes (page 246) and sautéed green beans and portobello mushrooms (see sidebar on page 251).

**SERVING SUGGESTION:** Add real mashed potatoes.

## I SAY FLANK STEAK, YOU SAY ROUND STEAK

✳ Okay, so you go to the store with your trusty grocery list, ready to round up some flank steak in the refrigerated meat section. What do your eyeballs see? Big $$$! Eek, you can't do that or your budget will be blown from here to South America. What's a gal to do?

Substitute! There is nothing that says you must have only flank steak or you will go to low-carb prison for changing an ingredient. As a matter of fact, round steak, which is gentle on the budget and will keep you from blowing a financial gasket, is a great stand-in for flank steak. The neat thing is that the round steak will tenderize nicely, too, because all of the flank steak recipes in this book call for a marinade, so you won't be put in a tough situation—literally!

# ❄ Week Five

**DAY ONE:** Pan-Seared Salmon with Lemon-Sage Butter
**DAY TWO:** Cube Steaks with Rich, Sweet Onion Gravy
**DAY THREE:** Skillet Chicken Mediterranean
**DAY FOUR:** Thai Shrimp on Red and Green Cabbage
**DAY FIVE:** Polka-Dot Meat Loaf
**DAY SIX:** Carolina Crock Pork

## SHOPPING LIST

### MEAT

4 boneless, skinless chicken breast halves
4 salmon fillets
1½ pounds large raw shrimp, peeled and deveined
4 cube steaks
1½ pounds ground turkey
1½ pounds pork shoulder roast

### CONDIMENTS

olive oil
vegetable oil
low-sodium soy sauce
vinegar (if not using wine)
cider vinegar
rice vinegar
Worcestershire sauce
barbecue sauce (you'll need ⅓ cup)
**lc Dijon mustard
**lc mayonnaise
**salad dressing—your choice

## PRODUCE

3 pounds onions (keep on hand)

1 red onion

1 head garlic; **1 extra

1 tomato

1 bunch cilantro (you'll need ½ cup)

red cabbage (you'll need 2 cups)

green cabbage (you'll need 2 cups)

1 red bell pepper (you'll need ⅓ cup)

8 ounces mushrooms; **lc extra (1 meal)

1 lemon (you'll need 1 tablespoon lemon juice)

**lc 1 bag spinach

**1 bag coleslaw mix

**lc 1–2 heads lettuce (*not* iceberg) (2 meals)

**lc 1 bunch Swiss chard

**lc 2–3 heads cauliflower (3 meals)

**lc Brussels sprouts (1 meal)

**lc green beans (1 meal)

**lc salad veggies (2 meals)

**russet potatoes (1 meal)

**red potatoes (1 meal)

**sweet potatoes (1 meal)

## CANNED GOODS

1 14½-ounce can beef broth

1 can corn (you'll need ⅓ cup)

1 6-ounce can tomato paste

1 jar roasted red peppers (you'll need ¼ cup)

1 jar marinated artichoke hearts (you'll need 1 cup)

1 jar kalamata olives (you'll need ¼ cup)

1 jar salsa

**SPICES**

crushed red pepper

chili powder

cumin

dry mustard

garlic powder

sage

thyme

**DAIRY/DAIRY CASE**

butter

2 eggs

**lc low-fat shredded Cheddar cheese

**lc 2 8-ounce packages cream cheese (2 meals)

**milk

**DRY GOODS**

whole-wheat flour

¼ cup dry-roasted peanuts

**1 pound brown rice

**1 package angel hair pasta (1 meal)

**BAKERY**

1 loaf low-carb whole-wheat bread (you'll need 2 slices)

**whole-wheat hamburger buns

**OTHER**

white wine (you'll need ¼ cup, if not using white grape
   juice)

white grape juice (you'll need ¼ cup, if not using white
   wine)

# PAN-SEARED SALMON WITH LEMON-SAGE BUTTER

*Serves 4*

*1 tablespoon olive oil*
*Salt and pepper to taste*
*4 salmon fillets*
*4 tablespoons butter, softened*
*1 teaspoon sage, crumbled*
*1 teaspoon lemon juice*

In a skillet, heat olive oil over medium-high heat. Salt and pepper the fish well on both sides and add to the pan. Make sure pan has been heated well before adding.

While salmon is cooking, place butter, sage, and lemon juice in a small bowl and, using a small whisk, whip together well. When fish has finished cooking (3 to 5 minutes each side), dollop a tablespoon of the Lemon-Sage Butter on each fillet and serve.

PER SERVING
330 Calories; 21g Fat (57.5% calories from fat); 34g Protein; trace Carbohydrate; trace Dietary Fiber; 119mg Cholesterol; 231mg Sodium. Exchanges: 0 Grain (Starch); 5 Lean Meat; 0 Fruit; 3 Fat.

NOTE: To cut fat grams in half, use whipped butter instead and cut amount back by a tablespoon.

LC SERVING SUGGESTIONS: Braised Swiss chard (see sidebar on page 254) and Baked Cheesy Cauliflower (page 247).

SERVING SUGGESTION: Add brown rice.

(see sidebar on page 254) (page 247)

## FISHING FOR COMPLIMENTS

❋ If you're wondering why the fish is rarely specified (salmon would be an exception) in these recipes, it's because fish is tough to dictate. There are too many possibilities for problems. For some, it's a regional, availability thing; for others, the choice is based on affordability; and still for others, it's the convenience factor—there are bags of frozen generic white fish that can be picked up at the market and be done with it.

Fish, whether it's fresh, frozen, from fresh water, or from the ocean—if it had gills during its lifetime, it will work in these recipes, I promise.

# CUBE STEAKS WITH RICH, SWEET ONION GRAVY

*Serves 4*

*4 cube steaks*
*Salt and pepper to taste*
*1 teaspoon thyme*
*2 tablespoons olive oil, divided*
*1 large onion, cut into slices*
*1 cup beef broth, divided*
*1 tablespoon whole-wheat flour*

Season steaks with salt and pepper and thyme on both sides. In a large skillet, heat half the olive oil over medium-high heat. Brown the steaks on both sides, about 3 minutes each side. Remove from pan and keep warm.

Add the remaining olive oil, heat, and then add the onion. Cook till the onion becomes translucent; then add half the broth, deglaze the pan with your wire whisk (get up all the browned bits off the bottom), and let simmer about 5 minutes to reduce slightly. Place the steaks right on top of the onion, cover, and simmer on low for about 5 minutes. Then remove beef and onion and keep warm. Turn up the heat and continue heating remaining liquid in the pan.

Take the remaining beef broth and mix it with the flour. Pour into the sauce, stirring till thickened. To serve, place steak on the plate, top with onion, and then ladle gravy over the top.

**PER SERVING**
296 Calories; 20g Fat (62.1% calories from fat); 23g Protein; 7g Carbohydrate; 2g Dietary Fiber; 63mg Cholesterol; 375mg Sodium. Exchanges: 0 Grain (Starch); 3 Lean Meat; ½ Vegetable; 2 Fat.

**LC SERVING SUGGESTIONS:** Serve with Mashed Faux-tay-toes (page 246) and add steamed Brussels sprouts and sautéed mushrooms.

**SERVING SUGGESTION:** Add mashed potatoes.

# SKILLET CHICKEN MEDITERRANEAN

*Serves 4*

*2 tablespoons olive oil, divided*
*4 boneless, skinless chicken breast halves*
*½ red onion, sliced*
*2 cloves garlic, pressed*
*8 ounces mushrooms, sliced*
*½ cup diced tomato*
*¼ cup roasted red peppers, diced (from a jar, freeze the rest)*
*1 cup marinated artichoke hearts, drained and chopped*
*¼ cup white wine (or white grape juice with a splash of vinegar)*
*¼ cup kalamata olives*

In a skillet, heat half the olive oil over medium-high heat and brown the chicken well on both sides, about 10 minutes total. Chicken should be nearly cooked. Place in a 275-degree F oven, covered, to keep warm.

Into the skillet add the remaining olive oil and heat. Add the onion and garlic and cook till onion starts to get translucent. Add the mushrooms and tomatoes and cook for a minute. Now add the remaining ingredients and cook till hot and fragrant. Serve chicken with this mixture heaped on the top.

**PER SERVING**
302 Calories; 15g Fat (41.3% calories from fat); 31g Protein; 11g Carbohydrate; 4g Dietary Fiber; 68mg Cholesterol; 508mg Sodium. Exchanges: 4 Lean Meat; 2 Vegetable; 0 Fruit; 2 Fat.

**LC SERVING SUGGESTION:** Add Sautéed Garlicky Spinach (page 253).

**SERVING SUGGESTION:** Add roasted red potatoes.

# THAI SHRIMP ON RED AND GREEN CABBAGE

Serves 4

*2 cups red cabbage, shredded*
*2 cups green cabbage leaves, shredded*
*2 tablespoons vegetable oil, divided*
*1 tablespoon rice vinegar*
*1 onion, chopped*
*4 cloves garlic, pressed*
*1½ pounds large raw shrimp, peeled and deveined*
*2 teaspoons crushed red pepper*
*½ cup cilantro, chopped*
*4 tablespoons low-sodium soy sauce*
*¼ cup peanuts, dry-roasted and crushed*

In a wok or skillet heat 1 tablespoon of oil over medium-high heat; when it is hot, add the cabbage, half of each at a time, cooking it in batches. When cooked (tender, but not too soggy), place in a large mixing bowl. Toss with rice vinegar and set aside, keeping warm. The cabbage will be the bed on which you arrange the shrimp.

Back to the wok or skillet, add the remaining oil and heat over medium-high heat. Add the onion first and cook 1 minute. Now add the garlic, cooking another minute. Finally, add the shrimp and cook all together until the shrimp turns pink, about 3 to 4 minutes.

Add remaining ingredients, except peanuts, and cook till incorporated, less than 15 seconds. Serve on bed of cabbage with the peanuts sprinkled over the top.

**PER SERVING**
372 Calories; 18g Fat (43.4% calories from fat); 40g Protein; 13g Carbohydrate; 3g Dietary Fiber; 259mg Cholesterol; 948mg Sodium. Exchanges: ½ Grain (Starch); 5 Lean Meat; 1½ Vegetable; 3 Fat; 0 Other Carbohydrates.

**LC SERVING SUGGESTION**: Add a green salad.

**SERVING SUGGESTION**: This is good served on angel hair pasta, too.

# POLKA-DOT MEAT LOAF

*Serves 4*

1½ pounds ground turkey
1 teaspoon chili powder
1 teaspoon cumin
1 teaspoon garlic powder
Salt and pepper to taste
⅓ cup corn, drained
1 medium onion, chopped
¼ cup soft whole-wheat bread crumbs
2 eggs, slightly beaten
⅓ cup red bell pepper, chopped
⅓ cup barbecue sauce
Salsa

Preheat oven to 375 degrees F.

Place turkey in a large mixing bowl. Add spices and salt and pepper, and combine. Add corn, onion, bread crumbs, eggs, bell pepper, and barbecue sauce, mixing lightly but thoroughly, using *clean hands* (it's the only way to do meat loaf). Shape turkey mixture into big blobby blimp and place on a baking sheet (with sides). Bake for an hour or until cooked through. Cut loaf into slices and serve with warmed salsa.

Or, for less cooking time (at same oven temperature), use a muffin tin. Lightly grease the muffin cups and fill to brims with meat-loaf mixture. Bake for about 35 minutes or until cooked through.

**PER SERVING**
344 Calories; 17g Fat (45.9% calories from fat); 34g Protein; 11g Carbohydrate; 2g Dietary Fiber; 228mg Cholesterol; 820mg Sodium. Exchanges: ½ Grain (Starch); 4½ Lean Meat; ½ Vegetable; ½ Fat; 0 Other Carbohydrates.

LC SERVING SUGGESTIONS: Mashed Faux-tay-toes (page 246) and steamed green beans (see sidebar on page 251).

SERVING SUGGESTION: Add baked sweet potatoes.

# CAROLINA CROCK PORK

1 tablespoon olive oil
1½ pounds pork shoulder roast
½ cup onion, chopped
1 clove garlic, pressed
1 teaspoon dry mustard
Salt and pepper to taste
¼ cup tomato paste
¼ cup Worcestershire sauce
2 tablespoons cider vinegar

In a skillet, heat the olive oil and brown the pork roast on all sides. Place in a Crock-Pot with remaining ingredients. Cook on high for 5 to 7 hours or on low for 8 to 9 hours, depending on the type of slow cooker you have. When done, shred with two forks and serve with Crock-Pot juices.

PER SERVING
380 Calories; 27g Fat (63.4% calories from fat); 24g Protein; 11g Carbohydrate; 1g Dietary Fiber; 91mg Cholesterol; 507mg Sodium. Exchanges: 0 Grain (Starch); 3 Lean Meat; 1 Vegetable; 3½ Fat; ½ Other Carbohydrates.

LC SERVING SUGGESTIONS: Serve with Basic Coleslaw (page 255). Add a big green salad.

SERVING SUGGESTIONS: Serve on whole-wheat hamburger buns with a good barbecue sauce and Basic Coleslaw (page 255), too. If you're from the South or wish you were, put the pork and slaw directly on the bun and chow down.

# ❄ Week Six

**DAY ONE:** The Ultimate Chicken Stir-Fry

**DAY TWO:** Creole Salmon Cakes

**DAY THREE:** Cabbage Roll Soup

**DAY FOUR:** Winter Spinach Salad with Turkey

**DAY FIVE:** RECIPE RAVE: Pork Medallions with a Creamy Wine Sauce

**DAY SIX:** Crock-Pot Taco Meat

## SHOPPING LIST

### MEAT

4 boneless, skinless chicken breast halves

8 turkey breast cutlets (about a pound)

1½ pounds pork tenderloins (about 2 whole), cut into rounds (medallions)

1 pound salmon (if not using frozen or canned)

1 pound round steak

1 pound extra-lean ground beef

### CONDIMENTS

vegetable oil

sesame oil

vinegar (if not using white wine)

teriyaki sauce

Worcestershire sauce

Italian salad dressing (Paul Newman's Balsamic Vinaigrette is great!)

**lc salad dressing—your choice

**lc rice vinegar

**lc mayonnaise

**tartar sauce

## PRODUCE

3 pounds onions (keep on hand)

1 red onion (you'll need ½ cup)

gingerroot (you'll need 4 tablespoons)

1 head garlic

1 bunch green onions (you'll need 4) **lc extra

1 bunch parsley (you'll need 1 tablespoon)

1 red bell pepper

1 green bell pepper

bean sprouts (you'll need 3 cups)

bok choy (you'll need 2 cups)

snow peas (you'll need 1½ cups)

mushrooms (you'll need 1 pound + 1½ cups)

½ head cabbage

1 10-ounce bag pre-washed spinach

**lc 1–2 heads lettuce (*not* iceberg) (3 meals)

**lc 1 head romaine lettuce (if not using tortillas)

**lc kale (1 meal)

**lc 1 head cauliflower (1 meal)

**lc salad veggies (3 meals)

**lc cilantro (garnish)

**rutabaga (1 meal)

**1 bag coleslaw mix

**russet potatoes (1 meal)

## CANNED GOODS

1 1-pound can salmon, drained (if not using fresh or frozen)

1–2 cans tomatoes (you'll need 1 cup chopped + 1 14½-ounce can)

2 14½-ounce cans Mexican-style stewed tomatoes (Rotell is a good brand)

2 14½-ounce cans chicken broth

1 jar capers (you'll need 2 tablespoons)

**1 can beans (black beans or refried beans are good) (1 meal)

SPICES
basil
white pepper
chili powder
garlic powder

DAIRY/DAIRY CASE
butter
1 egg
half-and-half (you'll need ⅔ cup)
sour cream (you'll need 4 tablespoons) **lc extra for 2
    meals
sharp Cheddar cheese—optional (you'll need 1–2 cups)
**lc 1 cup cheese (choose from blue, Feta, Cheddar, or Swiss)
**lc Cheddar cheese (or blend) for tacos
**lc 8-ounce package cream cheese

DRY GOODS
brown sugar
seasoned bread crumbs (you'll need ¼ cup)
1 package taco seasoning mix
**2–3 pounds brown rice (3 meals)

FROZEN FOODS
1-pound salmon (if not using fresh or canned)

BAKERY
**lc low-carb tortillas
**tortillas
**whole-wheat hamburger buns
**whole-grain rolls (2 meals)

OTHER
white wine (you'll need ⅔ cup, if not using white grape juice)
white grape juice (you'll need ⅔ cup, if not using white wine)

# THE ULTIMATE CHICKEN STIR-FRY

*Serves 4*

*4 boneless, skinless chicken breast halves, cut into strips*
*4 tablespoons teriyaki sauce*
*4 green onions, chopped*
*3 cups bean sprouts*
*2 cups bok choy, chopped*
*1½ cups snow peas*
*1½ cups mushroom, sliced*
*2 tablespoons vegetable oil*
*4 cloves garlic, pressed*
*4 tablespoons gingerroot, grated*
*1 tablespoon sesame oil*

First things first: Place the chicken in a large, zipper-topped plastic bag and add the teriyaki sauce. Squish it around to completely coat and place in the fridge. Now prep all your veggies.

In a very large skillet or (better) wok, heat vegetable oil over medium-high heat. Add garlic and ginger, heating till fragrant (just a minute).

Add the chicken half at a time so it cooks thoroughly. Pull from the wok when done and keep warm.

Now add the rest of the veggies, stir-frying constantly to make sure they don't burn. Add the sesame oil at this point. This should take about 5 minutes of cooking, depending on the size of your veggies, of course.

Add back the chicken and the accumulated juices to the wok and cook another 2 minutes or so, until all is incorporated, fragrant, and wonderful. Serve as is.

**PER SERVING**
289 Calories; 12g Fat (37.2% calories from fat); 33g Protein; 13g Carbohydrate; 3g Dietary Fiber; 68mg Cholesterol; 799mg Sodium. Exchanges: 4 Lean Meat; 2½ Vegetable; 2 Fat.

**LC SERVING SUGGESTION:** A big green salad.

**SERVING SUGGESTION:** Serve on a bed of brown rice.

# CREOLE SALMON CAKES

*Serves 4*

1 1-pound can salmon, drained (or you can use cooked salmon,
   fresh or frozen)
1 egg, slightly beaten
1 medium onion, finely diced
½ green bell pepper, finely diced
1 cup canned tomatoes, drained and chopped
3 tablespoons butter
¼ cup seasoned bread crumbs
1 tablespoon parsley, chopped
Salt and pepper to taste
1 teaspoon garlic powder
1 teaspoon chili powder

1 or 2 cups shredded sharp Cheddar cheese

Preheat oven to 375 degrees F.

In a saucepan, mix together salmon and egg. Add finely diced onion
and green pepper, tomatoes, butter, bread crumbs, parsley, salt and pepper, garlic powder, and chili powder. Simmer this mixture together
slowly about 10 minutes. Let cool and form into 4 salmon cakes.

Place in a lightly greased pan and bake for 10 more minutes. Top
with cheese; bake 5 minutes or until cheese is melted. Serve and enjoy.

PER SERVING
305 Calories; 17g Total Fat (50% calories from fat); 26g Protein; 2g Dietary Fiber; 11g Carbohydrate; 132mg Cholesterol; 1152mg Sodium. Exchanges: ½ Grain (Starch); 2½ Lean Meat;
1 Vegetable; 0 Fruit; 2 Fat; 0 Other Carbohydrates.

LC SERVING SUGGESTIONS: Rutabaga Fries (page 249) and some Basic
Coleslaw (page 255).

SERVING SUGGESTION: Throw the salmon cake on a bun and serve with
tartar sauce.

# CABBAGE ROLL SOUP

*Serves 4*

1 pound extra-lean ground beef
1 onion, chopped
Salt and pepper to taste
1 14½-ounce can tomatoes
½ head cabbage, shredded
1 tablespoon brown sugar
½ tablespoon Worcestershire sauce
4 cloves garlic, pressed
2 14½-ounce cans chicken broth
4 tablespoons sour cream

In a large saucepan, brown beef with the onion, and salt and pepper to taste. Blot any grease with paper toweling.

Add the rest of the ingredients, except the sour cream, and bring to a boil. Turn heat down, cover the soup, and let simmer for about 10 minutes or until the cabbage is tender.

Serve with a dollop of sour cream on top and enjoy!

**PER SERVING**
350 Calories; 23g Fat (60.5% calories from fat); 25g Protein; 9g Carbohydrate; 1g Dietary Fiber; 85mg Cholesterol; 490mg Sodium. Exchanges: 3½ Lean Meat; 1 Vegetable; 0 Non-Fat Milk; 2½ Fat; 0 Other Carbohydrates.

**LC SERVING SUGGESTION:** Serve with a big green salad.

**SERVING SUGGESTIONS:** Add cooked brown rice (¼ cup per bowl) and some whole-grain rolls.

# WINTER SPINACH SALAD WITH TURKEY

*Serves 4*

*5 tablespoons Italian salad dressing, divided (I like Paul Newman's
    Balsamic Vinaigrette)*
*8 turkey breast cutlets, cut into strips (about 1 pound)*
*1 teaspoon basil*
*Salt and pepper to taste*
*1 pound mushrooms, sliced, divided*
*1 cup red bell pepper, cut into strips*
*½ cup red onion, chopped*
*1 10-ounce bag pre-washed spinach, torn (or use baby spinach and
    don't tear)*

In a large skillet over medium-high heat, heat 2 tablespoons of the
dressing. Add turkey, basil, and salt and pepper to taste; brown, stirring
occasionally, until cooked through, about 5 minutes. Remove turkey
and set aside, keeping warm.

In the same skillet, heat 1 tablespoon more of the dressing, then add
half the mushrooms, the bell pepper, and onion; cook, stirring frequently, until mushrooms just begin to release their liquid and soften
up, about 3 minutes.

In a large salad bowl, combine spinach and remaining mushrooms;
add cooked mushroom mixture, turkey, and remaining 2 tablespoons of
dressing, tossing together well.

**PER SERVING**
271 Calories; 11g Fat (35.7% calories from fat); 31g Protein; 14g Carbohydrate; 4g Dietary
Fiber; 66mg Cholesterol; 280mg Sodium. Exchanges: 3½ Lean Meat; 2½ Vegetable; 0 Fruit;
2 Fat.

**LC SERVING SUGGESTION:** For a more substantial meal, add 1 cup crumbled cheese (blue or Feta) or shredded Cheddar or Swiss.

**SERVING SUGGESTION:** Add whole-grain rolls.

## * Recipe Rave:
## PORK MEDALLIONS WITH A
## CREAMY WINE SAUCE

*Serves 4*

"Pork Medallions with a Creamy Wine Sauce is *outstanding!*"

—RHEBA

"Pork Medallions with a Creamy Wine Sauce. Scrumptious."

—MONICA

1½ pounds pork tenderloins (*about 2 whole*), *cut into rounds*
  (*medallions*)
2 tablespoons butter
Dash olive oil
Salt and pepper to taste
⅔ cup white wine (*or white grape juice with a splash of*
  *vinegar*)
⅔ cup half-and-half
1 clove garlic, pressed
⅛ teaspoon white pepper
2 tablespoons capers, drained

In a large skillet over medium heat, melt butter (with a dash of olive oil to keep it from burning) and cook pork medallions about 3 to 4 minutes on each side. Salt and pepper to taste. Remove pork and keep warm.

For the sauce: Add wine to skillet drippings. Bring to a boil and, using a wire whisk, scrape up any browned bits in the skillet. Now lower the heat (*important*) and add the half-and-half, garlic, and white pepper. Cook and stir 3 minutes or until reduced—don't bring to a boil or the sauce will break. Remove from heat, and stir in capers. To serve, pour sauce over pork.

**PER SERVING**
285 Calories; 10g Total Fat (37% calories from fat); 37g Protein; trace Dietary Fiber; 2g Carbohydrate; 126mg Cholesterol; 276mg Sodium. Exchanges: 0 Grain (Starch); 5 Lean Meat; 0 Vegetable; 0 Fruit; 1 Fat; 0 Other Carbohydrates.

**LC SERVING SUGGESTIONS:** Serve with Mashed Faux-tay-toes (page 246) and braised kale (see sidebar on page 254).

**SERVING SUGGESTION:** Use real mashed potatoes as well.

# CROCK-POT TACO MEAT

*Serves 4*

*1 pound round steak, whacked into chunks to fit your Crock-Pot*
*1 package taco seasoning mix (or 2 tablespoons of my homemade taco seasoning blend; see sidebar on page 9)*
*2 14½-ounce cans Mexican-style stewed tomatoes (Rotell is a good brand)*

Throw everything into a Crock-Pot. Cook for 6 to 8 hours on low or 2 to 4 hours on high, depending on the type of slow cooker you have. Take two forks and shred beef to serve. Keep the sauce, too . . . delicious!

PER SERVING
259 Calories; 14g Total Fat (49% calories from fat); 23g Protein; 2g Dietary Fiber; 9g Carbohydrate; 67mg Cholesterol; 774mg Sodium. Exchanges: 0 Grain (Starch); 3 Lean Meat; ½ Vegetable; 0 Fruit; 1 Fat; ½ Other Carbohydrates.

LC SERVING SUGGESTIONS: Serve in La Tortilla Factory's low-carb tortillas and make burritos. Add cheese, chopped cilantro, sour cream, and chopped green onions; throw a salad on the side, and you're there. No low-carb tortillas? No problem. Use romaine lettuce leaves and roll 'em up!

SERVING SUGGESTIONS: Regular tortillas for your non-low-carbers. Add beans and brown rice, too, if you like.

## BOASTING ABOUT ROASTING

※ High-temperature roasting is a method of cooking that I came across quite by accident. I was making roast chicken for dinner and had forgotten to put the bird in the oven. I decided I'd speed things up a bit and threw the thing in at 475 degrees F. My reasoning was that I'd turn it down a bit later and we'd have a late dinner instead of a midnight feast.

Well, lo and behold, as fate would have it, I completely forgot about blitz cooking my poor little bird, and, in less than an hour, it was near perfection. I couldn't believe my eyes when I found the sweet thing golden, fragrant, and nearly ready to pull out of the oven. Surely it will be raw on the inside, I thought. Wrong! It was truly one of the best chickens I had ever made.

So years later, when I stumbled upon Barbara Kafka's classic *Roasting: A Simple Art,* I was thrilled to see that my mistake was a bona fide cooking method! Now, not only do I roast at high temps when I'm busy, I do it when I'm not busy, too. It is simply the best way to get a juicy, succulent, tasty roasted piece of meat or fowl, and it totally helps those of us in a need of a quick meal, too.

# SPRING

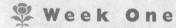

# Week One

**DAY ONE:** Mexican Chicken Skillet
**DAY TWO:** Bistro Salmon
**DAY THREE:** Oven-Roasted Marinated Flank Steak
**DAY FOUR:** Low-Carb Italian Wedding Soup
**DAY FIVE:** Turkey Picadillo
**DAY SIX:** Crock Pork Jambalaya

## SHOPPING LIST

### MEAT
8 chicken breast tenders
1 pound flank steak
1 pound ground turkey
4 boneless pork chops
4 salmon fillets
½ pound Italian sausage
½ pound kielbasa

### CONDIMENTS
olive oil
vegetable oil
balsamic vinegar
low-sodium soy sauce

### PRODUCE
3 pounds onions (keep on hand)
1 head garlic

1 bunch green onions

1 green bell pepper

3 red bell peppers

1–2 tomatoes (you'll need 1 cup)

3 zucchini (you'll need 2 + 1 cup)

1 small carrot

celery (you'll need 2 stalks)

spinach (you'll need 1 cup); **lc extra (2 meals)

kale (you'll need 2 cups)

**lc 1–2 heads lettuce (*not* iceberg) (2 meals)

**lc 1 head cauliflower (1 meal)

**lc salad veggies (2 meals)

**lc green beans (1 meal)

**lc Brussels sprouts (1 meal)

**lc mushrooms (1 meal)

**lc turnips (2 meals)

**lc rutabagas (1 meal)

** red potatoes (1 meal)

**russet potatoes (1 meal)


## CANNED GOODS

2 14½-ounce cans chicken broth (you'll need 1 can + ½
cup)

1 14½-ounce can stewed tomatoes

1 14½-ounce can tomatoes

1 4-ounce can tomato sauce

1 jar salsa (you'll need 1 cup)

**1 can black beans (1 meal)


## SPICES

chili powder

Cajun seasoning

cayenne pepper—optional

bay leaf

ground cumin

garlic powder

oregano

marjoram

red pepper flakes

rosemary

## DAIRY/DAIRY CASE

**lc Romano cheese (garnish)

**lc 8-ounce package cream cheese

**butter

**milk

## DRY GOODS

brown sugar

**2 pounds brown rice (3 meals)

## FROZEN FOODS

1 bag whole-kernel corn (you'll need ½ cup)

## BAKERY

**whole-grain rolls

## OTHER

white wine—optional

# MEXICAN CHICKEN SKILLET

*1 tablespoon olive oil, plus 2 teaspoons*
*8 chicken breast tenders*
*1 teaspoon chili powder*
*1 teaspoon ground cumin*
*1 teaspoon garlic powder*
*½ cup green bell pepper strips*
*½ cup red bell pepper strips*
*1 onion, thinly sliced*
*½ cup frozen whole-kernel corn*
*1 cup salsa—your favorite*

In a skillet, heat the 1 tablespoon of olive oil over medium-high heat. Add chicken and stir-fry 3 minutes. Stir in all 3 spices. Remove chicken from skillet and set aside.

Add remaining oil to skillet, and heat over medium-high heat. Add the green and red bell pepper and onion, stir-frying together for about 3 minutes.

Return the chicken to the skillet and stir in the corn and salsa. Stir-fry 2 minutes longer or until all is thoroughly heated.

**PER SERVING**
347 Calories; 17g Total Fat (43% calories from fat); 36g Protein; 3g Dietary Fiber; 13g Carbohydrate; 100mg Cholesterol; 380mg Sodium. Exchanges: ½ Grain (Starch); 5 Lean Meat; 1½ Vegetable; 0 Fruit; 1 Fat; 0 Other Carbohydrates.

**LC SERVING SUGGESTION:** A big salad is all you really need.

**SERVING SUGGESTIONS:** You can add brown rice and black beans.

# BISTRO SALMON

*Serves 4*

*2 tablespoons olive oil, divided*
*4 salmon fillets*
*½ cup sliced onion*
*2 garlic cloves, pressed*
*1 cup chopped zucchini*
*¼ cup sliced celery*
*½ cup diced red bell pepper*
*1 teaspoon dried oregano*
*1 cup diced tomato*
*1 teaspoon dried rosemary*
*1 cup chopped spinach*
*Salt and pepper to taste*

Heat half the oil in a large skillet over medium-high heat. Cook fish fillets on both sides, remove from the pan, and keep warm. Add remaining oil, heat, and then add the onion, garlic, zucchini, celery, bell pepper, and oregano and sauté 2 minutes. Stir in the tomato and rosemary; cook an additional 2 minutes. Stir in spinach and salt and pepper to taste; cook 1 minute or until spinach wilts. Top fish with this mixture and serve.

**PER SERVING**
268 Calories; 12g Fat (40.7% calories from fat); 32g Protein; 8g Carbohydrate; 2g Dietary Fiber; 81mg Cholesterol; 154mg Sodium. Exchanges: 0 Grain (Starch); 4 Lean Meat; 1 Vegetable; 2 Fat.

**LC SERVING SUGGESTIONS:** Serve with sautéed green beans (see sidebar on page 251) and oven-roasted garlicky turnips. (Peel and quarter turnips, toss in a little olive oil, sprinkle with garlic powder and salt and pepper. Bake in a 425-degree F oven for 10 minutes one side, turn, and bake another 10 minutes, assuming the turnips are smallish, of course.)

**SERVING SUGGESTIONS:** Add quartered red potatoes to the turnips and roast with all together. See Oven-Roasted Rutabagas (page 249). Pull them out separately and serve the taters to your carb-eating family.

**DO-AHEAD TIP:** Marinate flank steak for tomorrow night's dinner.

# OVEN-ROASTED
# MARINATED FLANK STEAK

*Serves 4*

**WARNING:** This recipe uses a high-temperature cooking method and requires you to preheat the pan. DO NOT USE A GLASS BAKING DISH FOR THIS RECIPE; it will shatter!

> ¼ *cup balsamic vinegar*
> ¼ *cup vegetable oil*
> 2 *tablespoons brown sugar*
> 2 *tablespoons low-sodium soy sauce*
> 4 *green onions, chopped (divided; reserve half for garnish)*
> 2 *cloves garlic, pressed*
> *Pepper to taste*
> 1 *pound flank steak*

Mix all ingredients (except beef) in a large, zipper-topped plastic bag. Stab the beef all over, and then place the beef in the bag. Mush it around until well covered. Refrigerate overnight.

Preheat oven to 500 degrees F.

Place a stainless baking pan (about a 13- × 9-inch one) in the bottom third of the oven and allow the metal pan to heat up for 10 minutes. Then add the meat, including the marinade, to the hot metal pan. For medium rare, roast the flank steak for about 7 minutes. Turn it and then roast for 7 minutes more. Slice thinly and serve with chopped green onions over the top.

**PER SERVING**
272 Calories; 20g Fat (67.5% calories from fat); 17g Protein; 5g Carbohydrate; trace Dietary Fiber; 55mg Cholesterol; 437mg Sodium. Exchanges: 0 Grain (Starch); 2½ Lean Meat; 0 Vegetable; 2½ Fat; ½ Other Carbohydrates.

**LC SERVING SUGGESTIONS:** Sautéed spinach and Rutabaga Fries (page 249).

**SERVING SUGGESTION:** Add brown rice.

# LOW-CARB ITALIAN WEDDING SOUP

*Serves 4*

*½ pound Italian sausage, casing removed*
*1 small onion, diced*
*2 cloves garlic, pressed*
*2 cups kale, chopped*
*1 14½-ounce can chicken broth*
*2 zucchini, chopped*
*½ teaspoon oregano*
*½ teaspoon marjoram*
*½ teaspoon salt*
*Dash crushed red-pepper flakes to taste*

In a large heavy saucepan brown sausage over medium-high heat. Stir in onion and garlic; cook and stir until soft, about 2 minutes. Now add the kale and cook another 3 minutes. Stir in remaining ingredients; bring to a boil, lower heat, and simmer for about 8 to 10 minutes. Soup should be quite thick.

**PER SERVING**
359 Calories; 19g Fat (47.7% calories from fat); 17g Protein; 11g Carbohydrate; 6g Dietary Fiber; 43mg Cholesterol; 1562mg Sodium. Exchanges: 1 Grain (Starch); 1½ Lean Meat; 2 Vegetable; 3 Fat.

**LC SERVING SUGGESTIONS:** Serve with a big green salad. Top soup with grated Romano cheese.

**SERVING SUGGESTION:** Add whole-grain rolls.

# TURKEY PICADILLO

*1 pound ground turkey*
*1 tablespoon olive oil*
*1 small onion, chopped*
*1 clove garlic, pressed*
*½ small red bell pepper, chopped*
*½ small carrot, finely chopped*
*¼ cup white wine—optional*
*1 tablespoon balsamic vinegar*
*½ bay leaf*
*Salt and pepper to taste*
*1 14½-ounce can stewed tomatoes, undrained*
*1 4-ounce can tomato sauce*

Cook turkey in a large skillet over medium-high heat until browned, breaking it up as you go. Drain; then blot well with paper towels to reduce fat grams. Remove from pan.

Add oil to pan. Add onion and garlic, sautéing for about 2 minutes. Add bell pepper and carrot; sauté for an additional 2 minutes. Add back the turkey, then stir in the remaining ingredients. Bring to a boil. Reduce heat and simmer for about 15 minutes, stirring occasionally. Remove bay leaf before serving.

**PER SERVING**
362 Calories; 23g Fat (58.4% calories from fat); 23g Protein; 13g Carbohydrate; 3g Dietary Fiber; 78mg Cholesterol; 467mg Sodium. Exchanges: 3 Lean Meat; 2½ Vegetable; 0 Fruit; 2½ Fat.

**LC SERVING SUGGESTIONS:** Serve over Mashed Faux-tay-toes (page 246), and add steamed Brussels sprouts and sautéed mushrooms.

**SERVING SUGGESTION:** Add mashed potatoes.

# CROCK PORK JAMBALAYA

*Serves 4*

1 tablespoon olive oil

4 boneless pork chops, cut into 1-inch cubes (trim fat for fewer fat grams)

Salt and pepper to taste

½ pound kielbasa, sliced

1 14½-ounce can tomatoes, with juice

½ red bell pepper, chopped

½ cup chicken broth

1 teaspoon oregano

1 teaspoon Cajun seasoning

¼ teaspoon cayenne pepper, for an extra-hot kick—optional

1 onion, chopped

1 stalk celery, chopped

In a skillet, heat olive oil; salt and pepper the pork chops and brown evenly on all sides. Place the browned pork at the bottom of the Crock-Pot, then add remaining ingredients. Cook on low for 7 hours, depending on the type of slow cooker you have.

PER SERVING
361 Calories; 22g Fat (56.4% calories from fat); 31g Protein; 8g Carbohydrate; 2g Dietary Fiber; 105mg Cholesterol; 977mg Sodium. Exchanges: 0 Grain (Starch); 4 Lean Meat; 1 Vegetable; 2 Fat; 0 Other Carbohydrates.

LC SERVING SUGGESTIONS: Serve on a bed of spinach. The heat from the pork will wilt the spinach nicely and make for a satisfying meal. Add some Turnip Fries (page 248).

SERVING SUGGESTION: Add some brown rice.

## HOMEMADE CAJUN SEASONING

You don't have to buy this stuff if you don't want to. Here's a simple recipe for making up your own Cajun seasoning:

2 teaspoons white pepper

2 teaspoons garlic powder

2 teaspoons onion powder

2 teaspoons cayenne pepper

2 teaspoons paprika

2 teaspoons black pepper

Mix everything together and keep in a sealed container.

# Week Two

**DAY ONE:** Broiled Greek Shrimp

**DAY TWO:** RECIPE RAVE: Cube Steaks with Blue Cheese

**DAY THREE:** Szechwan Turkey on Spinach

**DAY FOUR:** Many-Herbed Roasted Salmon

**DAY FIVE:** Easy Chicken Chili

**DAY SIX:** Leanne's Basic Crock Veggie Soup

## SHOPPING LIST

### MEAT

2 pounds large raw shrimp, peeled and deveined

4 salmon fillets

6 boneless, skinless chicken breast halves

8 turkey cutlets

4 cube steaks

### CONDIMENTS

olive oil

vegetable oil

**lc salad dressing—your choice

### PRODUCE

3 pounds onions (keep on hand)

1 small red onion

2 medium red bell peppers

2 jalapeno peppers—optional

celery (you'll need 3 stalks)

2 large carrots

1 medium turnip

2 heads garlic

1 piece gingerroot (you'll need 1 tablespoon)

1–2 lemons (you'll need 2 tablespoons juice)

1 lime (you'll need about 1 tablespoon juice)

1 head cabbage (you'll need ¼ head)

1 bunch cilantro (you'll need 2 tablespoons)

1 bunch fresh Italian parsley (you'll need ½ cup + extra for garnish)

1–2 bags spinach (you'll need 8 cups); **lc extra (1 meal)

snow peas (you'll need 1 cup)

2 cups green beans

2 russet potatoes; **extra (1 meal)

**lc 2–3 heads lettuce (*not* iceberg) (3 meals)

**lc 2 heads cauliflower (2 meals)

**lc kale (1 meal)

**lc spaghetti squash (1 meal); **(1 meal)

**lc salad veggies (3 meals)

**lc zucchini (1 meal)

**lc yellow squash (1 meal)


## CANNED GOODS

3 14½-ounce cans diced tomatoes

1 28-ounce can tomatoes

4 14½-ounce cans or 1 48-ounce can chicken broth

**1 can corn (1 meal)

**1 can white beans (1 meal)


## SPICES

thyme

basil

cumin

ground coriander

cayenne pepper

ground pepper

crushed red pepper

## DAIRY/DAIRY CASE

crumbled Feta cheese (you'll need 1 cup)

blue cheese crumbles (4 tablespoons)

orange juice (you'll need ¼ cup, if not buying frozen)

butter

**lc 8-ounce package cream cheese

**sour cream (garnish) (2 meals)

**lc low-fat Cheddar cheese (about 1 cup)

**lc cheese for grilled quesadillas—your choice (Mexican blend, Cheddar, etc.)

## DRY GOODS

cornstarch

** 2–3 pounds brown rice (3 meals)

## FROZEN FOODS

orange juice (you'll need ¼ cup, if not buying fresh)

## BAKERY

**lc low-carb tortillas (1 meal)

**regular tortillas or loaf of bread (1 meal)

**corn-bread muffins (1 meal)

## OTHER

dry sherry—optional (you'll need 2 tablespoons)

# BROILED GREEK SHRIMP

*Serves 4*

*1 tablespoon olive oil*
*5 garlic cloves, pressed*
*1 14½-ounce can diced tomatoes, drained*
*½ cup chopped fresh Italian parsley, divided*
*2 pounds large raw shrimp, peeled and deveined*
*1 cup crumbled Feta cheese*
*2 tablespoons fresh lemon juice*
*¼ teaspoon fresh ground pepper*

Preheat broiler.

In a skillet over medium heat, heat the olive oil. Add garlic and sauté for 30 seconds. Add tomatoes and half the parsley. Reduce heat; simmer 10 minutes. Add shrimp and cook for 5 minutes. Pour mixture into a broiler-proof baking dish and sprinkle with Feta cheese. Broil till nicely melted and slightly brown on top. Watch as it broils. It takes only a second!

Before serving, sprinkle with parsley, lemon juice, and pepper.

**PER SERVING**
400 Calories; 15g Total Fat (35% calories from fat); 53g Protein; 1g Dietary Fiber; 11g Carbohydrate; 378mg Cholesterol; 917mg Sodium. Exchanges: 0 Grain (Starch); 7 Lean Meat; 1 Vegetable; 0 Fruit; 2 Fat; 0 Other Carbohydrates.

**LC SERVING SUGGESTIONS:** Serve on a bed of baked spaghetti squash with a big green salad.

**SERVING SUGGESTIONS:** Serve on brown rice with spaghetti squash on the side.

## ❦ Recipe Rave:
## CUBE STEAKS WITH BLUE CHEESE

*Serves 4*

"The Cube Steaks with Blue Cheese has to qualify for a recipe rave. My husband asks for it about twice a week!"

—JACKIE

> *4 cube steaks*
> *Salt and pepper to taste*
> *4 tablespoons crumbled blue cheese*
> *⅛ cup red onion, finely chopped*

Preheat broiler.

Meanwhile, in a skillet, brown cube steaks to your liking, and salt and pepper to taste. Blot grease off meat and place in a broiler pan.

Top each steak with blue cheese and red onion. Stick under the broiler to melt and serve.

**PER SERVING**
238 Calories; 16g Fat (60.9% calories from fat); 22g Protein; 1g Carbohydrate; trace Dietary Fiber; 70mg Cholesterol; 172mg Sodium. Exchanges: 3 Lean Meat; 0 Vegetable; 1 Fat.

**LC SERVING SUGGESTIONS:** Sautéed zucchini and yellow squash, and a big green salad. (Watch the carb count on your salad dressings; dressings higher in fat usually have lower carb counts.)

**SERVING SUGGESTION:** Add baked potatoes.

# SZECHWAN TURKEY ON SPINACH

*Serves 4*

¼ cup orange juice

¼ cup water

2 tablespoons dry sherry—optional

½ teaspoon crushed red pepper

8 turkey cutlets

1 tablespoon vegetable oil, divided

1 medium red bell pepper, cut into strips

1 cup snow peas

1 tablespoon fresh gingerroot, grated

2 teaspoons cornstarch

8 cups spinach

Italian parsley, chopped

In a large, zipper-topped plastic bag, combine orange juice, water, sherry, and crushed red pepper. Place turkey in bag, mush around, and refrigerate while you prep your veggies.

Heat half the oil in a skillet. Add bell pepper, snow peas, and ginger. Stir-fry for 2 minutes. Remove from skillet and keep warm.

Add remaining oil to the skillet. Drain turkey, reserving the marinade. Stir-fry the turkey till cooked, about 4 to 5 minutes, depending on the thickness of the cutlets. Remove the turkey from the skillet and add to the veggies. Keep warm.

Add the cornstarch to the marinade, mix well, and add to the skillet. Cook, stirring constantly, until thickened. Add the veggies and turkey back in and cook for just another 1 or 2 minutes to get everything mixed together and heated.

Immediately serve atop a bed of fresh spinach. The heat from the turkey will wilt the spinach just right. Garnish with Italian parsley.

**PER SERVING**
187 Calories; 7g Total Fat (36% calories from fat); 21g Protein; 1g Dietary Fiber; 7g Carbohydrate; 53mg Cholesterol; 52mg Sodium. Exchanges: 0 Grain (Starch); 3 Lean Meat; ½ Vegetable; 0 Fruit; ½ Fat; 0 Other Carbohydrates.

**LC SERVING SUGGESTION:** Sautéed garlic cauliflower.

**SERVING SUGGESTION:** Add brown rice.

# MANY-HERBED ROASTED SALMON

*1 tablespoon olive oil*
*1 tablespoon butter, melted*
*4 salmon fillets*
*½ teaspoon basil*
*¼ teaspoon thyme*
*Salt and pepper to taste*
*½ cup onion, finely chopped*

Preheat oven to 475 degrees F.

In a roasting pan, place the oil and melted butter. Roll the salmon in it till well coated. Sprinkle the herbs, salt and pepper, and chopped onion all over the top.

Roast the fish in the oven for about 5 minutes, then turn and finish cooking (another 3 to 5 minutes, depending on how thick the fillets are). The fish is done when it flakes easily with a fork. Don't overcook.

**PER SERVING**
261 Calories; 12g Fat (43.1% calories from fat); 34g Protein; 2g Carbohydrate; trace Dietary Fiber; 96mg Cholesterol; 144mg Sodium. Exchanges: 0 Grain (Starch); 5 Lean Meat; ½ Vegetable; 1½ Fat.

**LC SERVING SUGGESTIONS:** Serve with Mashed Faux-tay-toes (page 246) and braised kale (see sidebar on page 254).

**SERVING SUGGESTION:** Add brown rice.

**DO-AHEAD TIP:** Pre-cook chicken for tomorrow's dinner.

# EASY CHICKEN CHILI

*Serves 4*

*2 tablespoons olive oil*

*1 large onion, chopped*

*4 cloves garlic, pressed*

*1 stalk celery, chopped*

*1 red bell pepper, seeded, deribbed, and chopped*

*2 jalapeno peppers, seeded, deribbed, and chopped—optional*

*1–2 teaspoons ground cumin*

*2 teaspoons ground coriander*

*½ teaspoon cayenne pepper*

*Salt and pepper to taste*

*1 28-ounce can tomatoes, broken up*

*6 boneless, skinless chicken breast halves, cooked and chopped into*
  *1-inch pieces*

*Juice of 1 lime*

*2 tablespoons fresh cilantro, chopped*

In a large saucepan or skillet, heat oil over medium heat. Sauté onion, garlic, celery, peppers, seasonings, and salt and pepper over medium-low heat for about 5 minutes.

Add tomatoes. Simmer gently for 20 minutes. Stir in cooked chicken and cook until heated through. Before serving, add lime juice and fresh cilantro and stir gently.

### PER SERVING
283 Calories; 13g Fat (41.1% calories from fat); 31g Protein; 11g Carbohydrate; 3g Dietary Fiber; 82mg Cholesterol; 273mg Sodium. Exchanges: 0 Grain (Starch); 4 Lean Meat; 2 Vegetable; 1 Fat.

LC SERVING SUGGESTIONS: Serve in bowls and top with low-fat Cheddar cheese and a blop of sour cream. Serve with a big green salad.

SERVING SUGGESTIONS: Add a can of drained white beans and 1 cup drained canned corn for a more "chili" meal. Serve also with corn-bread muffins.

# LEANNE'S BASIC CROCK
# VEGGIE SOUP

*Serves 12 (freezes great, or makes
a terrific leftover for the weekend)*

*1 large onion, chopped*
*4 cloves garlic, pressed*
*2 tablespoons olive oil, divided*
*2 large carrots, chopped*
*2 small celery stalks, chopped*
*1 medium turnip, chopped*
*2 cups green beans, chopped into 1-inch pieces*
*¼ head cabbage, chopped*
*2 small russet potatoes, peeled and chopped*
*6 cups chicken broth*
*2 14½-ounce cans diced tomatoes, undrained*
*½ teaspoon thyme*
*Salt and pepper to taste*

In a large soup pot, heat 1 tablespoon of the olive oil over medium-high heat. Add the onion and cook till nearly translucent, then add the garlic. Don't let the garlic brown while sautéing for another couple of minutes.

Add the rest of the chopped veggies, sautéing for just 1 or 2 minutes. You're not cooking them, just sautéing for the wonderful flavor this quick step will infuse in your soup. Add the thyme and salt and pepper while sautéing.

Now put the veggies in the Crock-Pot, and add the tomatoes and broth. Cook on low 7 to 9 hours or high 4 to 6 hours, depending on the type of slow cooker you have. When the veggies are tender, and the soup smells delicious, it is ready. Gently mash some of the potatoes on the side of the Crock-Pot to slightly thicken the soup, and give it a stir before serving.

PER SERVING
88 Calories; 4g Total Fat (35% calories from fat); 5g Protein; 2g Dietary Fiber; 9g Carbohydrate; 0mg Cholesterol; 658mg Sodium. Exchanges: 0 Grain (Starch); ½ Lean Meat; 1 Vegetable; 0 Fruit; ½ Fat; 0 Other Carbohydrates.

**LC SERVING SUGGESTIONS:** Serve with low-carb quesadillas and a big spinach salad. To make quesadillas, think grilled cheese sandwiches made with low-carb tortillas (use La Tortilla Factory's wonderful low-carb tortillas).

**SERVING SUGGESTIONS:** Regular quesadillas or grilled cheese sandwiches.

## Week Three

**DAY ONE:** Chinese Beef and Broccoli

**DAY TWO:** Crustless Quiche Lorraine

**DAY THREE:** Herbed Skillet Pork Chops

**DAY FOUR:** RECIPE RAVE: Cajun Salmon

**DAY FIVE:** Ritzy Crab Casserole

**DAY SIX:** Southwest Crock Chicken

### SHOPPING LIST

#### MEAT

1 pound boneless sirloin or round steak

4 pork chops, about ½ inch thick

8 boneless, skinless chicken thighs

4 4-ounce salmon fillets

5 ounces crab meat (about 1 cup) (if not using frozen or canned)

8 turkey bacon slices

#### CONDIMENTS

olive oil

vegetable oil

sesame oil

low-sodium soy sauce

dry sherry (you'll need 1 tablespoon)—optional

balsamic vinegar (¼ cup, if not using vermouth wine)

**salad dressing—your choice

#### PRODUCE

3 pounds onions (keep on hand)

1 head garlic

1 piece gingerroot (you'll need 1 teaspoon)

1–2 lemons

1 large red bell pepper

2 medium zucchini

broccoli (you'll need 1 pound flowerets); **lc 1 head
(1 meal)

mushrooms (you'll need 2 cups)

1 bunch parsley (you'll need 2 tablespoons)

1 bunch cilantro (topping)—optional

**lc 2–3 heads lettuce (3 meals)

**lc 2–3 bags spinach (3 meals)

**lc 1–2 heads cauliflower (2 meals)

**lc spaghetti squash (1 meal)

**lc salad veggies (3 meals)

**lc green beans (1 meal)

**lc yellow string beans (1 meal)

**Yukon gold potatoes (1 meal)

## CANNED GOODS

2 14½-ounce cans chicken broth

apple juice (you'll need ¼ cup, if not using vermouth)—
optional

5 ounces crab meat (about 1 cup, if not using frozen or
fresh)

1 jar salsa (you'll need ¾ cup)

## SPICES

cumin

thyme

garlic powder

onion powder

white pepper

cayenne pepper

Cajun seasoning

**DAIRY/DAIRY CASE**

butter

6 eggs

half-and-half (you'll need 1½ cups)

Swiss cheese (1 cup shredded)

skim milk, or any other milk you have (you'll need 1 cup)

sour cream (topping)—optional

**lc Romano cheese (garnish)

**DRY GOODS**

cornstarch

whole-wheat flour

**1 package noodles (egg noodles or angel hair is good; any style will work okay)

**2–3 pounds brown rice (3 meals)

**FROZEN FOODS**

5 ounces crab meat (about 1 cup, if not using fresh or canned)

**OTHER**

vermouth (you'll need ½ cup, if not using apple juice)

# CHINESE BEEF AND BROCCOLI

*Serves 4*

*1 pound boneless sirloin or round steak, cut into 2-inch strips*
*1 pound broccoli, cut into flowerets, steamed till tender*
*1 tablespoon plus 1 teaspoon vegetable oil, divided*
*Dash white pepper*
*6 cloves garlic, pressed*
*1 teaspoon gingerroot, grated*
*1 cup mushrooms, sliced*
*1 teaspoon cornstarch*
*1 teaspoon low-sodium soy sauce*
*¼ cup chicken broth*
*1 teaspoon sesame oil*

While prepping your beef to stir-fry, steam your broccoli.

In a skillet or wok, heat 1 tablespoon oil. Then add beef and a dash of white pepper, stir-frying till browned, about 3 minutes or less. Remove beef and keep warm. Next add the garlic, gingerroot, and mushrooms; stir-fry again for about 2 minutes. Put remaining vegetable oil in skillet, add back the beef, and add the steamed broccoli.

Mix together the cornstarch with soy sauce and chicken broth, mixing till lumpless. Stir cornstarch mixture into skillet; cook and stir about 30 seconds or until thickened. During the last 30 seconds of cooking, add the sesame oil. Serve and enjoy!

PER SERVING
227 Calories; 11g Total Fat (42% calories from fat); 27g Protein; 1g Dietary Fiber; 7g Carbohydrate; 66mg Cholesterol; 201mg Sodium. Exchanges: 0 Grain (Starch); 3½ Lean Meat; 1 Vegetable; 0 Fruit; 1 Fat; 0 Other Carbohydrates.

LC SERVING SUGGESTIONS: Serve on a bed of baked spaghetti squash with a green salad on the side.

SERVING SUGGESTION: Add brown rice.

# CRUSTLESS QUICHE LORRAINE

*Serves 4*

*8 turkey bacon slices, cooked and chopped*
*1 cup shredded Swiss cheese*
*1 medium onion, chopped*
*2 tablespoons whole-wheat flour*
*4 eggs*
*1 cup skim milk, or any other milk you have*
*Salt and pepper to taste*
*⅛ teaspoon cayenne pepper (for an extra little bite)—optional*

Heat oven to 350 degrees F.

Lightly grease a 9-inch pie plate. Toss the bacon, cheese, onion, and flour together and spread in the bottom of the pie plate.

In a bowl, beat eggs together first, then beat in milk and add cayenne pepper, salt, and pepper to taste. Pour egg mixture over bacon mixture. Bake uncovered 35 to 40 minutes or until knife inserted in center comes out clean. Let stand 10 minutes before cutting.

**PER SERVING**
286 Calories; 18g Total Fat (56% calories from fat); 21g Protein; 2g Dietary Fiber; 10g Carbohydrate; 239mg Cholesterol; 930mg Sodium. Exchanges: 0 Grain (Starch); 2½ Lean Meat; ½ Vegetable; 0 Fruit; 2 Fat; 0 Other Carbohydrates.

**LC SERVING SUGGESTION/SERVING SUGGESTION:** Serve with a big spinach salad.

# HERBED SKILLET PORK CHOPS

*Serves 4*

½ teaspoon thyme

1 teaspoon garlic powder

½ teaspoon onion powder

Salt and pepper to taste

4 pork chops, about ½ inch thick

1 tablespoon olive oil

½ cup plus 1 tablespoon water, divided

1 tablespoon cornstarch

2 tablespoons chopped parsley

Combine thyme, garlic powder, onion powder, and salt and pepper; sprinkle over chops. In a skillet, heat olive oil over medium heat; add pork chops and cook 10 minutes or until slightly browned, turning once. Remove pork and keep warm, add ½ cup water to the skillet and, using a wire whisk, scrape the pan to get up all the browned bits. Bring water to a boil and add chops back in; cover, reduce heat, and cook 10 to 20 minutes, depending on thickness of chops, until pork is done. Remove chops from skillet. Combine cornstarch and remaining 1 tablespoon water. Add to pan juices; cook until thickened and translucent, stirring or whisking constantly. Pour sauce over chops and sprinkle with parsley.

PER SERVING

202 Calories; 13g Fat (57.9% calories from fat); 19g Protein; 3g Carbohydrate; trace Dietary Fiber; 40mg Cholesterol; 632mg Sodium. Exchanges: 0 Grain (Starch); 2½ Lean Meat; 0 Vegetable; 1 Fat.

LC SERVING SUGGESTIONS: Sautéed green beans (see sidebar on page 251) and a big green salad. (Watch the carb count on your salad dressings. Dressings higher in fat usually have lower carb counts.)

SERVING SUGGESTIONS: Follow LC Suggestion above and add brown rice.

## NO PIGGING OUT

Some people don't eat pork for religious reasons, or have declared their homes—for whatever reason—to be pork-free zones. That doesn't smoke my bacon one bit, but I do have a solution for you, rather than skipping the recipe.

Substitute a little poultry instead. Honestly, chicken breasts do the trick for pork chop recipes just fine. And for the stir-fry pork recipes? How about some turkey breast, cut in strips?

You don't have to take it in the chops just because you don't do pork. Just chicken out instead—it works great.

## ❧ Recipe Rave:
# CAJUN SALMON

*Serves 4*

"My husband thanks you by the way. He fell in love with the Cajun Salmon, so I know this is going to be a favorite in our house! We were never fish eaters, but with recipes like these, we will be now!"

—JENNIE

> 2 tablespoons butter
> 4 4-ounce salmon fillets
> 2 tablespoons Cajun seasoning
> 2 cloves garlic, pressed
> ½ cup vermouth (or ¼ cup each balsamic vinegar and apple juice,
>     mixed)
> Lemon wedges

In a large skillet over medium-high heat, melt half the butter. Add the salmon and brown on each side, about 2 minutes per side. Remove salmon and keep warm. Add remaining butter to the pan, and add Cajun seasoning and garlic. Cook for 2 minutes, stirring constantly. Then add the vermouth and cook for 3 minutes or so, again stirring constantly. Add salmon back to the pan and cook until fish flakes when tested with a fork. Serve with lemon wedges.

**PER SERVING**
243 Calories; 10g Fat (43.9% calories from fat); 23g Protein; 5g Carbohydrate; 1g Dietary Fiber; 74mg Cholesterol; 466mg Sodium. Exchanges: 3 Lean Meat; 0 Vegetable; 1 Fat; 0 Other Carbohydrates.

**LC SERVING SUGGESTIONS:** Steamed cauliflower topped with grated Romano cheese, and steamed baby spinach.

**SERVING SUGGESTION:** Add steamed Yukon gold potatoes.

# RITZY CRAB CASSEROLE

*Serves 4*

*¼ cup butter*
*¼ cup finely chopped onion*
*1 cup mushrooms, sliced*
*3 tablespoons whole-wheat flour*
*1½ cups half-and-half*
*2 egg yolks, slightly beaten*
*5 ounces crab meat (about 1 cup), fresh, frozen, or canned*
*1 tablespoon dry sherry—optional*
*Dash cayenne pepper*
*Salt and pepper to taste*

In a skillet, heat butter and sauté onions and mushrooms until tender. Stir in flour; cook and stir 1 minute. Add half-and-half; cook and stir about 5 minutes or until thickened. Stir a small amount of hot mixture into yolks; now add yolks to hot mixture (important: combining this way will prevent your "scrambling" the egg). Stir in the crab, sherry, and cayenne; salt and pepper to taste. Cook and stir until crab is thoroughly heated.

**PER SERVING**
251 Calories; 18g Fat (63.9% calories from fat); 12g Protein; 11g Carbohydrate; 2g Dietary Fiber; 171mg Cholesterol; 271mg Sodium. Exchanges: ½ Grain (Starch); 1 Lean Meat; ½ Vegetable; ½ Non-Fat Milk; 3 Fat.

**LC SERVING SUGGESTIONS:** Serve on a bed of raw (preferably baby) spinach. The heat will adequately wilt the spinach. Serve a side of sautéed yellow string beans.

**SERVING SUGGESTION:** Serve on a bed of buttered noodles.

# SOUTHWEST CROCK CHICKEN

*Serves 4*

*1 tablespoon vegetable oil*
*8 boneless, skinless chicken thighs*
*Salt and pepper to taste*
*1 14½-ounce can chicken broth*
*¾ cup salsa*
*1 large red bell pepper, cut into 1-inch pieces*
*2 medium zucchini, cut in half lengthwise and sliced crosswise so*
  *¾ inch thick*
*1½ teaspoons ground cumin*
*2 tablespoons cornstarch*
*¼ cup water*


*Sour cream—optional*
*Chopped fresh cilantro—optional*


In a skillet, heat oil over medium-high heat until hot. Add chicken (½ at a time) and cook till nice and browned. Remove from the skillet, season with salt and pepper, and place the chicken on the bottom of the crockery insert.

In the same skillet, combine the broth, salsa, bell pepper, zucchini, and cumin. Bring to a boil, then reduce the heat to medium-low for just a minute. Now add all of this to the top of the chicken.

Cook for about 7 hours on low, depending on the type of slow cooker you have. At the last hour of cooking, dissolve cornstarch in ¼ cup water and add mixture to Crock-Pot; keep the lid off the Crock-Pot to help it thicken. Otherwise, place the cooking liquid in a large saucepan and cook on the stovetop at a medium heat till it has thickened slightly.

PER SERVING
322 Calories; 12g Total Fat (45% calories from fat); 23g Protein; 2g Dietary Fiber; 12g Carbohydrate; 72mg Cholesterol; 747mg Sodium. Exchanges: ½ Grain (Starch); 3 Lean Meat; 1½ Vegetable; 0 Fruit; 2 Fat; 0 Other Carbohydrates.

LC SERVING SUGGESTIONS: Serve with steamed broccoli and cauliflower, and a big green salad.

SERVING SUGGESTION: Add brown rice.

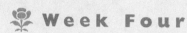
# Week Four

**DAY ONE:** Garlic Buffalo Turkey

**DAY TWO:** Baked Fish Picante

**DAY THREE:** Asian Chicken Stir-Fry

**DAY FOUR:** Skillet Seafood Stew

**DAY FIVE:** RECIPE RAVE: Spiced Pork Chops

**DAY SIX:** Big Bumpy Broccoli Soup

## SHOPPING LIST

### MEAT

1¼ pounds boneless, skinless chicken breast halves

8 turkey breast cutlets

4 pork chops

4 halibut or other lean fish steaks (about 1 inch thick)
(about 2 pounds)

½ pound fish fillet(s), in pieces

1 pound medium raw shrimp, peeled and deveined

### CONDIMENTS

olive oil

sesame oil

vinegar (if not using white wine)

balsamic vinegar

hoisin sauce

low-sodium soy sauce

Tabasco sauce

blue cheese salad dressing

**lc salad dressing—your favorite

### PRODUCE

3 pounds onions (keep on hand)

2 heads garlic (13 cloves)

1 piece gingerroot (you'll need 2 teaspoons grated)

1 lime (you'll need juice)

2 red bell peppers

1 cup snow-pea pods

2 jalapeno chilies—optional

1 bunch green onions (you'll need ½ cup)

1 bunch cilantro (you'll need 1 cup + garnish)

1 bunch broccoli; **lc 2–3 bunches extra (3 meals)

celery; **lc extra

1 small carrot

**lc 2–3 heads lettuce (*not* iceberg) (3 meals)

**lc red cabbage

**lc green cabbage

**lc 1 bag spinach (1 meal)

**lc salad veggies (3 meals)

**lc turnips (2 meals)

**lc spaghetti squash (1 meal)

**russet potatoes (1 meal)

## CANNED GOODS

2 14½-ounce cans whole tomatoes

2 14½-ounce cans low-sodium chicken broth

1 bottle or jar clam juice (you'll need 2 ounces or ¼ cup)

## SPICES

cayenne pepper

garlic powder

ground cumin

ground coriander

marjoram

oregano

paprika

fennel seeds

red pepper flakes

**DAIRY/DAIRY CASE**

butter

half-and-half (you'll need 1 cup)

**lc Cheddar cheese (garnish for soup)

**DRY GOODS**

cornstarch

peanuts (you'll need ¼ cup)

whole-wheat flour

**1 pound brown rice

**spaghetti or angel hair pasta noodles

**BAKERY**

**whole-grain rolls (2 meals)

**OTHER**

white wine (you'll need ½ cup, if not using white grape juice)

white grape juice (you'll need ½ cup, if not using white wine)

# GARLIC BUFFALO TURKEY

*Serves 4*

*3 cloves garlic, pressed*
*1 tablespoon butter*
*½ teaspoon cayenne, or to taste*
*1 teaspoon Tabasco sauce, or to taste*
*8 turkey breast cutlets, cut in half*
*2 tablespoons blue cheese salad dressing*

In a skillet, heat the butter over medium heat. Add the garlic, seasonings, and turkey. Stir-fry till turkey is cooked, about 5 minutes or so. If turkey starts to stick, add a teaspoon or so of vegetable oil. You should be okay, though.

Evenly distribute the turkey to each plate and drizzle blue cheese dressing on top to serve.

PER SERVING
225 Calories; 9g Fat (36.3% calories from fat); 34g Protein; 1g Carbohydrate; trace Dietary Fiber; 102mg Cholesterol; 439mg Sodium. Exchanges: 0 Grain (Starch); 5 Lean Meat; 0 Vegetable; 1½ Fat.

LC SERVING SUGGESTIONS: Serve with celery sticks, raw broccoli, and extra blue cheese dip, as well as a big green salad and some Turnip Fries (page 248).

SERVING SUGGESTION: Add some baby carrots and Real Oven Fries (page 249).

# BAKED FISH PICANTE

*Serves 4*

1 tablespoon olive oil

1 large onion, sliced

2 cloves garlic, pressed

2 jalapeno chilies, seeded and chopped—optional

1 16-ounce can whole tomatoes, drained and chopped

2 tablespoons balsamic vinegar

1¼ teaspoons ground cumin

¾ teaspoon ground coriander

4 halibut or other lean fish steaks, about 1 inch thick (about
   2 pounds)

Chopped fresh cilantro

Preheat oven to 350 degrees F.

In a skillet, heat the olive oil over medium heat and cook onion, garlic, and chilies (optional) stirring frequently, until onion is tender; reduce heat. Stir in remaining ingredients except the fish and cilantro. Simmer uncovered over low heat for 5 minutes, stirring occasionally.

Arrange fish in an ungreased baking dish. Spoon the tomato mixture over the fish and bake uncovered for 25 to 30 minutes or until fish flakes easily with fork. Sprinkle with cilantro.

PER SERVING
258 Calories; 8g Total Fat (27% calories from fat); 37g Protein; 9g Carbohydrate; 2g Dietary Fiber; 54mg Cholesterol; 262mg Sodium. Exchanges: 0 Grain (Starch); 5 Lean Meat; 1½ Vegetable; 0 Fruit; ½ Fat; 0 Other Carbohydrates.

LC SERVING SUGGESTIONS: Serve with Sautéed Garlicky Spinach (page 253) and steamed broccoli.

SERVING SUGGESTION: Add brown rice.

# ASIAN CHICKEN STIR-FRY

*Serves 4*

2 teaspoons sesame oil

1¼ pounds boneless, skinless chicken breast halves, cut into strips

4 cloves garlic, pressed

2 teaspoons gingerroot, grated

1 red bell pepper, cut into short, thin strips

1 cup snow-pea pods, washed and destringed (pull the stem and
    string off)

½ cup canned low-sodium chicken broth

1 teaspoon cornstarch

⅛ cup hoisin sauce

1 tablespoon low-sodium soy sauce

½ cup green onions, thinly sliced

¼ cup chopped peanuts

In a skillet, heat oil over medium-high heat until hot. Add chicken, garlic, and ginger, stir-frying for 3 minutes or until chicken is no longer pink. Transfer mixture to a bowl and set aside. Add bell pepper and snow peas to skillet; stir-fry 1 minute. Combine broth and cornstarch; mix well. Add broth mixture, hoisin sauce, and soy sauce to skillet; bring to a boil, stirring constantly. Add chicken mixture; stir-frying 1 minute more or until chicken is cooked through.

Spoon chicken mixture over "noodles" (see LC Serving Suggestion); sprinkle with green onions and peanuts and serve.

PER SERVING
283 Calories; 9g Fat (28.6% calories from fat); 38g Protein; 12g Carbohydrate; 3g Dietary Fiber; 83mg Cholesterol; 442mg Sodium. Exchanges: 0 Grain (Starch); 5 Lean Meat; 1 Vegetable; 1 Fat; 0 Other Carbohydrates.

LC SERVING SUGGESTION: Serve on a bed of spaghetti squash "noodles."

SERVING SUGGESTION: Skip the spaghetti squash and use regular cooked thin spaghetti noodles.

# SKILLET SEAFOOD STEW

*Serves 4*

*2 tablespoons olive oil*
*1 red bell pepper, sliced*
*1 onion, chopped*
*4 cloves garlic, pressed*
*¼ cup clam juice*
*½ cup white wine (or white grape juice with a splash of vinegar)*
*1 cup whole tomatoes, with juice*
*½ teaspoon red pepper flakes*
*Juice of 1 lime*
*½ pound fish fillet, in pieces*
*1 pound medium shrimp, peeled and deveined*
*1 cup chopped cilantro*

In a skillet, heat the olive oil over medium-high heat. Add the peppers, onion, and garlic and cook till nicely wilted and onion is translucent, about 8 minutes.

Add the clam juice, wine, tomatoes, red pepper flakes, and lime juice.

Now add the fish and shrimp, carefully cooking another 5 minutes until the fish is cooked through and easily flakes when tested with a fork and the shrimp is pink. Serve with chopped cilantro on top.

PER SERVING
292 Calories; 9g Fat (31.1% calories from fat); 34g Protein; 12g Carbohydrate; 2g Dietary Fiber; 197mg Cholesterol; 269mg Sodium. Exchanges: 0 Grain (Starch); 4½ Lean Meat; 1½ Vegetable; 0 Fruit; 1½ Fat; 0 Other Carbohydrates.

LC SERVING SUGGESTIONS: Serve on a bed of sautéed cabbage. Serve a big green salad on the side.

SERVING SUGGESTION: Serve with whole-grain rolls.

## ❦ Recipe Rave:
## SPICED PORK CHOPS

*Serves 4*

"I made Spiced Pork Chops and we took it over to eat with my father-in-law. The meal was declared 'restaurant quality . . . no—*better* than restaurant quality!' Thank you!"

—SUZAN

1 teaspoon paprika
½ teaspoon oregano
1 teaspoon cumin
1 teaspoon garlic powder
½ teaspoon salt
¼ teaspoon fennel seeds, crushed
⅛ teaspoon cayenne pepper
4 pork chops
1 tablespoon olive oil
½ tablespoon butter
½ cup chicken broth

Mix all spices together and evenly sprinkle half over the top of the pork chops. Then in a skillet over medium-high heat, heat olive oil. Place spiced side of the pork chops down in the hot skillet. Cook about 3 to 5 minutes on one side till browned (but not blackened; turn down the heat if they're cooking too fast). While chops are cooking on the first side, sprinkle remaining spice mixture on the uncooked side. Flip them over once; finish cooking.

Remove chops from skillet and keep warm. Add butter to skillet and whisk up browned bits with a wire whisk. Turn the heat up a little, add chicken broth, and keep whisking till the sauce reduces to about half. Serve the chops with the sauce on top.

PER SERVING
286 Calories; 20g Fat (63.8% calories from fat); 24g Protein; 1g Carbohydrate; trace Dietary Fiber; 78mg Cholesterol; 436mg Sodium. Exchanges: 0 Grain (Starch); 3½ Lean Meat; 2 Fat.

**LC SERVING SUGGESTIONS:** Serve with Oven-Roasted Turnips (page 248) and steamed broccoli.

**SERVING SUGGESTIONS:** Serve with baked potatoes as well as, or instead of, Oven-Roasted Turnips.

*Serves 4*

1 tablespoon olive oil
1 onion, chopped
2 cloves garlic, pressed
1 small stalk celery, chopped fine
1 small carrot, shredded
1 bunch broccoli, steamed
Salt and pepper to taste
½ teaspoon marjoram
1 14½-ounce can chicken broth
2 tablespoons whole-wheat flour
¼ cup cold water
1 cup half-and-half

In a skillet, heat the oil over medium-high heat. Add the onion, garlic, and the rest of the veggies to the skillet, except for the broccoli. Sauté for 5 minutes or until onion is translucent. Place the broccoli on the bottom of the Crock-Pot, followed by the sautéed veggies. Add everything else except the flour, water, and half-and-half. Let cook for 5 to 6 hours on low, depending on the type of slow cooker you have, or until everything is tender.

Remove some of the cooking liquid and place in a saucepan on the stovetop. Heat till nearly boiling.

Meanwhile, mix the flour and water in a small bowl with a fork or wire whisk until the flour is dissolved (I use a jar for this purpose and shake it violently). Pour this gradually into the cooking liquid on the stovetop, stirring constantly while pouring.

Heat to boiling over high heat, stirring constantly. Continue boiling 1 minute, stirring constantly (you may need to turn down the heat slightly to keep from scorching). Now it should be nice and thick.

To this mixture, stir in the half-and-half. Cook, stirring occasionally; you want it hot, NOT boiling. The soup should look hot and steamy and ready to boil, but do not let it boil or you will break your soup and have tiny bits of white clunky clotted milk solids in it. Not pretty. Add this back to the soup mixture in the Crock-Pot, stir well, and serve. You can smooth the soup out a bit in the blender or using one of the blending wands, or leave it big and bumpy, the way the recipe says.

PER SERVING
135 Calories; 8g Total Fat (53% calories from fat); 5g Protein; 2g Dietary Fiber; 11g Carbohydrate; 22mg Cholesterol; 499mg Sodium. Exchanges: 0 Grain (Starch); 0 Lean Meat; ½ Vegetable; 0 Fruit; 1½ Fat; 0 Other Carbohydrates.

LC SERVING SUGGESTIONS: Top with shredded Cheddar cheese, and serve with a big green salad.

SERVING SUGGESTION: Add some whole-grain rolls.

# Week Five

**DAY ONE:** Smothered Burgers
**DAY TWO:** Shrimp and Asparagus Stir-Fry
**DAY THREE:** Braised Pork Chops
**DAY FOUR:** Sausage and Peppers
**DAY FIVE:** Ginger-Curry Salmon
**DAY SIX:** Crock Chickie Chowder

## SHOPPING LIST

### MEAT

4 skinless chicken thighs
1 pound extra-lean ground beef
4 pork chops, about ½ inch thick
1 pound turkey sausage
4 salmon fillets, about 4 ounces each
1 pound medium raw shrimp, peeled and deveined (if not
buying frozen)

### CONDIMENTS

olive oil
honey
**lc mayonnaise
**lc Dijon mustard
**lc salad dressing—your choice

### PRODUCE

3 pounds onions (keep on hand)
2 heads garlic
1 piece gingerroot (you'll need 1 tablespoon grated)
1 bunch cilantro (you'll need ¼ cup)
1 small bell pepper (red or green)
2 medium red bell peppers

1 medium green bell pepper

2–3 bunches green onions (you'll need 1½ cups)

asparagus (you'll need 2 cups)

mushrooms (you'll need 1 cup, sliced)

1–2 limes (you'll need 2 tablespoons juice)

1–2 oranges (you'll need ¼ cup juice, if not buying frozen
  or in carton)

**lc 1 bag baby greens or spring mix of lettuces (1 meal)

**lc 1–2 bags spinach (2 meals)

**lc 1 bag coleslaw mix (1 meal)

**lc 1 head cauliflower (1 meal)

**lc broccoli (1 meal)

**lc red cabbage (1 meal)

**lc green cabbage (1 meal)

**lc salad veggies (2 meals)

**lc green beans

**lc turnips (1 meal)

**lc spaghetti squash

**russet potatoes (2 meals)

## CANNED GOODS

3 14½-ounce cans chicken broth

1 14½-ounce can diced tomatoes

1 jar green olives (you'll need ¼ cup)

## SPICES

curry powder

oregano

paprika

thyme

red pepper flakes

bay leaf

**lc garlic powder

### DAIRY/DAIRY CASE

orange juice (you'll need ¼ cup, if not making fresh or buying frozen)

half-and-half (you'll need ⅓ cup)

**lc low-fat shredded Cheddar cheese

**lc Romano cheese (garnish)

### DRY GOODS

**1–2 pounds brown rice (2 meals)

### FROZEN FOODS

1 pound medium raw shrimp, peeled and deveined (if not buying fresh)

orange juice (you'll need ¼ cup, if not making fresh or buying in carton)

1 10-ounce package frozen broccoli, green beans, pearl onions, and red peppers (or similar medley if your store doesn't have this one)

1 package frozen corn (you'll need ½ cup)

### BAKERY

**whole-grain rolls

# SMOTHERED BURGERS

*Serves 4*

*Salt and pepper to taste*
*1 pound extra-lean ground beef, shaped into 4 patties*
*1 tablespoon olive oil*
*1 onion, sliced*
*1 small bell pepper, cut into strips*
*1 cup mushrooms, sliced*
*2 cloves garlic, pressed*

Salt and pepper the hamburger patties to your taste.

In a skillet, heat the olive oil, and start sautéing the onion and bell pepper together. As onion begins to turn translucent, add the mushrooms and garlic. Salt and pepper to taste, and cook the veggie mixture until mushrooms are nicely cooked. Remove from skillet and keep warm.

In the same skillet, cook the burgers to your desired doneness, turning only once to encourage even browning.

Allow burgers to drain on a paper-towel-lined plate and reheat the veggies in the pan for just a minute. Then serve with veggies piled on top of the burgers.

PER SERVING
321 Calories; 23g Fat (64.9% calories from fat); 22g Protein; 6g Carbohydrate; 1g Dietary Fiber; 78mg Cholesterol; 77mg Sodium. Exchanges: 3 Lean Meat; 1 Vegetable; 2½ Fat.

LC SERVING SUGGESTIONS: Turnip Fries (page 248) and Basic Coleslaw (page 255).

SERVING SUGGESTION: Add Real Oven Fries (page 249).

# SHRIMP AND ASPARAGUS STIR-FRY

*Serves 4*

1 tablespoon olive oil

2 cups asparagus, cut diagonally

1 pound raw medium shrimp, peeled and deveined

1 cup green onions, chopped

2 cloves garlic, pressed

½ teaspoon oregano

¼ teaspoon red pepper flakes, or to taste

¼ cup orange juice

¼ cup chicken broth

¼ cup cilantro, chopped

In a skillet, heat the olive oil over medium-high heat. Add the asparagus and sauté till bright green, about 2 minutes. Add the shrimp, green onions, garlic, and spices. Cook till shrimp is nice and pink.

Add the juice and chicken broth and cook another minute. Remove the shrimp and asparagus and keep warm. Now increase the heat on the stovetop and whisk the sauce till reduced, about 2 minutes.

Return the shrimp mixture back to the sauce and cook another minute, completely incorporating the shrimp and sauce together. Sprinkle cilantro on top and serve.

**PER SERVING**
190 Calories; 6g Fat (26.8% calories from fat); 26g Protein; 9g Carbohydrate; 2g Dietary Fiber; 173mg Cholesterol; 225mg Sodium. Exchanges: 0 Grain (Starch); 3½ Lean Meat; 1 Vegetable; 0 Fruit; ½ Fat.

**LC SERVING SUGGESTIONS:** Serve this on a bed of sautéed cabbage. Add a salad of baby greens as well.

**SERVING SUGGESTION:** Serve on a bed of brown rice instead.

# BRAISED PORK CHOPS

*Serves 4*

1 tablespoon olive oil
Salt and pepper to taste
4 pork chops, about ½ inch thick
1 red bell pepper, cut in strips
½ onion, chopped
4 cloves garlic, pressed
1 14½-ounce can diced tomatoes, with juice
¼ cup green olives, cut in half
½ bay leaf
1 teaspoon paprika
½ teaspoon thyme

In a skillet over medium-high heat, heat the olive oil. Salt and pepper the pork chops, then brown in the hot oil, about 2 minutes each side.

Add the peppers, onion, and garlic and cook till onion is translucent, about 5 minutes. Add the tomatoes and the remaining ingredients, cover, and simmer for about 10 minutes or until pork chops are cooked through. Remember to remove the bay before serving.

**PER SERVING**
301 Calories; 19g Fat (58.0% calories from fat); 24g Protein; 7g Carbohydrate; 2g Dietary Fiber; 74mg Cholesterol; 138mg Sodium. Exchanges: 0 Grain (Starch); 3½ Lean Meat; 1 Vegetable; 0 Fruit; 2 Fat.

**LC SERVING SUGGESTIONS:** Serve with sautéed green beans (see sidebar on page 251) and Baked Cheesy Cauliflower (page 247).

**SERVING SUGGESTION:** Add baked potatoes.

# SAUSAGE AND PEPPERS

*Serves 4*

*1 tablespoon olive oil*
*1 pound turkey sausage, casings removed, cut diagonally in ½-inch*
   *pieces*
*1 onion, sliced thin*
*4 cloves garlic, pressed*
*1 red bell pepper, cut in strips*
*1 green bell pepper, cut in strips*

In a skillet, heat the olive oil over medium-high heat. Add the sausage, onion, garlic, and bell pepper and cook till onion is tender and sausage is cooked thoroughly. Serve.

**PER SERVING**
332 Calories; 26g Fat (67.9% calories from fat); 18g Protein; 9g Carbohydrate; 2g Dietary Fiber; 90mg Cholesterol; 766mg Sodium. Exchanges: 2½ Lean Meat; 1½ Vegetable; 3½ Fat.

**LC SERVING SUGGESTION:** Serve on a bed of spaghetti squash with Sautéed Garlicky Spinach (page 253) on the side (sprinkle a little Romano cheese on the top of the sausages, too).

**SERVING SUGGESTION:** Add some pasta and Romano cheese.

# GINGER-CURRY SALMON

> 2 tablespoons olive oil, divided
> Salt and pepper to taste
> 4 salmon fillets
> ½ cup green onions, chopped
> 1 tablespoon gingerroot, grated
> 2 tablespoons lime juice
> 1½ cups chicken broth
> 1 teaspoon curry powder
> 2 teaspoons honey

In a skillet, heat half the olive oil over medium-high heat. Sprinkle salt and pepper on fillets and add to skillet. Brown about 2 minutes on each side. Remove salmon and keep warm.

Add remaining oil and heat. Add the green onions and ginger, sautéing briefly. Now add the lime juice, chicken broth, and curry powder and simmer till sauce reduces a little, about 5 minutes. Next add the honey, and simmer again. Serve sauce over the top of the salmon.

**PER SERVING**
321 Calories; 17g Fat (47.4% calories from fat); 36g Protein; 5g Carbohydrate; 1g Dietary Fiber; 88mg Cholesterol; 403mg Sodium. Exchanges: 0 Grain (Starch); 5 Lean Meat; 0 Vegetable; 0 Fruit; 2 Fat; 0 Other Carbohydrates.

**LC SERVING SUGGESTION:** Serve with a big bunch of steamed broccoli.

**SERVING SUGGESTION:** Add brown rice.

# CROCK CHICKIE CHOWDER

1 tablespoon olive oil

½ onion, chopped

4 skinless chicken thighs, cut in 1 inch pieces

Salt and pepper to taste

2 cloves garlic, pressed

½ teaspoon thyme

1 cup chicken broth

10 ounces frozen broccoli, green beans, pearl onions, and red
    peppers, thawed (or similar medley if your store doesn't have this
    one)

½ cup frozen corn, thawed

⅓ cup half-and-half

In a skillet, heat olive oil over medium-high heat. Add onion and chicken and cook till chicken starts to brown, salting and peppering as you cook. Add the garlic and thyme and cook for an additional minute.

Empty the contents of the skillet into a Crock-Pot and add remaining ingredients except the half-and-half. Cook on low about 4 to 6 hours, depending on the type of slow cooker you have, or until chicken is cooked through and veggies are tender.

Turn the Crock-Pot to high; add the half-and-half, stirring well. Leave the lid off the Crock-Pot and let cook an additional 15 minutes or so (just long enough to make your salad and set the table).

Serve it up in bowls.

**PER SERVING**
195 Calories; 9g Fat (41.4% calories from fat); 17g Protein; 11g Carbohydrate; 2g Dietary Fiber; 65mg Cholesterol; 272mg Sodium. Exchanges: ½ Grain (Starch); 2 Lean Meat; 1 Vegetable; 0 Non-Fat Milk; 1 Fat.

**LC SERVING SUGGESTION:** Serve with a big spinach salad.

**SERVING SUGGESTION:** Add some whole-grain rolls.

## THE GREAT GREEN SALAD

Q: What should go in a big green salad?

A: Anything you want!

In the scheme of things, it doesn't really matter too much how much of a recipe you use or don't use to make your salads. The important thing is remembering that the color (or lack of color) is indicative of the nutrition it contains. In other words, the more colorful your salad, the more defined nutritionally it becomes.

Think in living color when you're buying the salad goodies for your salads.

- Red for tomatoes and red bell pepper, both high in vitamin C.
- Orange and yellow for carrot (higher in carbs, but a little goes a long way) and yellow summer squash grated into a salad is wonderful.
- Green, in the darker, more dramatic shades, indicates that you have something healthy going on in your lettuce leaves. Pale, washed-out iceberg is pretty much a washout nutritionally, too. Stick to the dark green leafies.

# Week Six

**DAY ONE:** Skillet Steaks with a Red Wine Sauce

**DAY TWO:** Oven-Baked Italian Fish

**DAY THREE:** Puerto Rican Turkey

**DAY FOUR:** Skillet Chops

**DAY FIVE:** Herb-Roasted Chicken Breasts

**DAY SIX:** Crocked BBQ Beef

## SHOPPING LIST

### MEAT

4 chicken breasts (with skin and bone)

8 turkey breast cutlets

4 rib-eye steaks (8 ounces each)

2 pounds rump roast (or other beef; rump is leaner cut)

4 pork chops (about ¾ inch thick)

4 fish fillets

4 pieces turkey bacon

### CONDIMENTS

olive oil

vinegar (if not using red wine)

balsamic vinegar

Worcestershire sauce

teriyaki sauce

Tabasco sauce

barbecue sauce (you'll need 10 ounces)

**lc mayonnaise

**lc salad dressing—your choice

### PRODUCE

3 pounds onions (keep on hand)

1 head garlic

mushrooms (you'll need 2 cups sliced)

1 red bell pepper

1 green bell pepper

cabbage (you'll need 4 cups shredded)

**lc asparagus (1 meal)

**lc broccoli (1 meal)

**lc 2 heads cauliflower (2 meals)

**lc green beans (1 meal)

**lc 1–2 heads lettuce (*not* iceberg) (3 meals)

**lc kale (1 meal)

**lc 1 bag spinach (1 meal)

**lc 1 bag coleslaw mix (1 meal)

**lc salad veggies (3 meals)

**lc green onions

**russet potatoes (1meal)

**red potatoes (1 meal)

**sweet potatoes (1 meal)

## CANNED GOODS

1 14½-ounce can beef broth

apple cider (you'll need 2 tablespoons)

## SPICES

oregano

rosemary

sage

thyme

garlic powder

onion powder

caraway seeds

## DAIRY/DAIRY CASE

butter

Romano cheese (you'll need 2 tablespoons)

**lc 2 8-ounce packages cream cheese (2 meals)
**lc eggs, you'll need to hard-boil

## DRY GOODS
seasoned bread crumbs (you'll need ¼ cup)
**1–2 pounds brown rice (2 meals)

## BAKERY
**whole-wheat hamburger buns

## OTHER
red wine (you'll need ½ cup, if not using red grape juice)
red grape juice (you'll need ½ cup, if not using red wine)

# SKILLET STEAKS WITH A RED WINE SAUCE

*Serves 4*

*4 rib-eye steaks (8 ounces each)*
*1 tablespoon butter*
*2 cloves garlic, pressed*
*2 cups mushrooms, sliced*
*Salt and pepper to taste*
*½ cup red wine (or red grape juice with a splash of vinegar)*
*1 tablespoon balsamic vinegar*
*1 tablespoon Worcestershire sauce*
*½ teaspoon thyme*
*¼ cup beef broth*

Heat the skillet over medium-high heat for 2 to 3 minutes, or until nice and hot (best not to use a nonstick skillet, if you can help it). Add the steaks to the skillet, searing well on both sides for about 3 to 5 minutes per side, depending on thickness. Remove steaks from the skillet and keep warm (they will continue to cook; if you want your meat rarer, you need less cooking time).

Add the butter to the skillet; then add the garlic and the mushrooms; salt and pepper to taste. Cook till the mushrooms begin to release their liquid and till soft and tender, but don't overcook. Remove and keep warm.

Now add the wine and remaining ingredients to the skillet and turn up the heat. Using a whisk, get the brown bits from the steaks up and cook till wine mixture has reduced to almost half. Add the mushrooms and their liquid back in and cook another minute; serve over the top of your steaks.

**PER SERVING**
355 Calories; 19g Fat (50.9% calories from fat); 37g Protein; 4g Carbohydrate; 1g Dietary Fiber; 91mg Cholesterol; 240mg Sodium. Exchanges: 0 Grain (Starch); 5 Lean Meat; ½ Vegetable; 0 Fruit; 1½ Fat; 0 Other Carbohydrates.

**LC SERVING SUGGESTION:** Serve with steamed asparagus.

**SERVING SUGGESTION:** Add baked potatoes.

# OVEN-BAKED ITALIAN FISH

*Serves 4*

*Salt and pepper to taste*
*4 fish fillets*
*½ teaspoon garlic powder*
*2 tablespoons Romano cheese, grated*
*¼ cup seasoned bread crumbs*
*2 tablespoons butter, melted*
*1 tablespoon olive oil*

Preheat oven to 400 degrees F. Salt and pepper the fish to taste, and sprinkle the garlic powder on fillets as well.

On a dinner plate, mix the cheese and bread crumbs together. In a little saucepan, melt butter and olive oil together.

Dip fish in the butter/oil mixture, and then dredge with the cheese/bread-crumb mixture. Place in a shallow baking pan.

Bake for about 10 to 15 minutes or until fish flakes easily when tested with a fork. Cooking time will vary, depending on the thickness of your fish.

**PER SERVING**
312 Calories; 12g Fat (35.1% calories from fat); 43g Protein; 6g Carbohydrate; trace Dietary Fiber; 119mg Cholesterol; 424mg Sodium. Exchanges: ½ Grain (Starch); 5½ Lean Meat; 2 Fat.

**LC SERVING SUGGESTIONS:** Steamed broccoli and green salad.

**SERVING SUGGESTION:** Add brown rice.

# PUERTO RICAN TURKEY

*Serves 4*

1 tablespoon olive oil, divided
1 onion, chopped
1 red bell pepper, cut in strips
1 green bell pepper, cut in strips
1 teaspoon oregano
4 pieces turkey bacon, chopped
8 turkey breast cutlets
Pepper to taste
1 tablespoon teriyaki sauce

In a skillet, heat half the olive oil over medium-high heat. Add the onion, peppers, oregano, and turkey bacon. Sauté for 4 minutes or so or until vegetables are tender. Remove from pan and keep warm.

Add remaining oil. Add turkey cutlets and cook quickly, peppering to taste. Add the teriyaki sauce and return reserved vegetables back to the skillet and cook till all is heated through and well incorporated. Serve.

**PER SERVING**
255 Calories; 8g Fat (29.4% calories from fat); 37g Protein; 7g Carbohydrate; 2g Dietary Fiber; 102mg Cholesterol; 679mg Sodium. Exchanges: 0 Grain (Starch); 5 Lean Meat; 1 Vegetable; 1 Fat.

**LC SERVING SUGGESTIONS:** Serve with Sautéed Garlicky Spinach (page 253) and some steamed green beans.

**SERVING SUGGESTION:** Add some red potatoes.

# SKILLET CHOPS

*Serves 4*

*2 tablespoons olive oil, divided*
*Salt and pepper to taste*
*4 pork chops, ¾ inch thick*
*2 cloves garlic, pressed*
*1 onion, sliced thin*
*4 cups shredded cabbage*
*1 teaspoon caraway seeds*
*2 tablespoons apple cider*

In a skillet, heat half the oil over medium-high heat. Salt and pepper the chops and add to the skillet. Brown well on both sides, about 5 minutes each side. Remove from pan and keep warm.

Add remaining oil, then add garlic, onion, and cabbage. Cook till wilted and cabbage shrinks up a bit, about 3 minutes (cabbage will shrink down a lot. You may need to do it in batches, or use a wok). Add the caraway seeds and cider and mix to incorporate. Now lay the chops on top of the cabbage mixture, cover, and reduce the heat to low and cook for another 10 to 20 minutes or until pork is cooked through. Check often to make sure you aren't burning it.

PER SERVING
327 Calories; 22g Fat (60.1% calories from fat); 25g Protein; 8g Carbohydrate; 2g Dietary Fiber; 74mg Cholesterol; 73mg Sodium. Exchanges: 3½ Lean Meat; 1½ Vegetable; 0 Fruit; 2½ Fat.

LC SERVING SUGGESTIONS: Serve with Mashed Faux-tay-toes (page 246) and a big green salad.

SERVING SUGGESTION: Add baked sweet potatoes.

DO-AHEAD TIP: Prepare herb marinade and marinate chicken overnight.

# HERB-ROASTED CHICKEN BREASTS

*Serves 4*

*4 chicken breasts (with skin and bone)*
*2 tablespoons olive oil*
*½ onion, chopped fine*
*2 cloves garlic, pressed*
*1 teaspoon thyme*
*½ teaspoon rosemary, crushed*
*¼ teaspoon oregano*
*¼ teaspoon sage*
*Salt and pepper to taste*
*1 shot Tabasco sauce*

In a large, zipper-topped plastic bag, place everything but the chicken. Mush it around to get everything well mixed, then add the chicken and mush it around again. At a minimum, you want the chicken marinating in this 4 hours, preferably overnight.

Preheat the oven to 425 degrees F.

Place chicken and marinade in a shallow roasting pan, skin side down, and cover with foil. Cook for 15 minutes. Remove foil, turn chicken so breast side is up, baste well with the juices, and cook again another 15 minutes or until nicely browned. Serve with pan juices.

**PER SERVING**
569 Calories; 34g Fat (54.5% calories from fat); 61g Protein; 2g Carbohydrate; 1g Dietary Fiber; 186mg Cholesterol; 217mg Sodium. Exchanges: 0 Grain (Starch); 8½ Lean Meat; ½ Vegetable; 1½ Fat.

**LC SERVING SUGGESTIONS:** Serve with braised kale (see sidebar on page 254) and a green salad.

**SERVING SUGGESTION:** Serve with brown rice.

# CROCKED BBQ BEEF

*Serves 4*

*1 tablespoon olive oil*
*2 pounds rump roast (or other beef; this cut is leaner)*
*Salt and pepper to taste*
*1 teaspoon garlic powder*
*1 teaspoon onion powder*
*10 ounces barbecue sauce, divided*

In a skillet, over medium-high heat, heat the olive oil. Add the roast and brown well on all sides. Remove roast and place in Crock-Pot.

Season roast with seasonings and salt and pepper, then top with half the barbecue sauce. Place the lid on and cook on low for 6 to 8 hours, depending on the type of slow cooker you have. When beef begins to shred easily, you're nearly there. Pull the beef and shred. Drain fat, but keep flavorful juices and add the shredded beef back in. Add remaining barbecue sauce, mix well, and cook for another hour to warm up.

PER SERVING
400 Calories; 16g Fat (36.6% calories from fat); 51g Protein; 10g Carbohydrate; 1g Dietary Fiber; 132mg Cholesterol; 707mg Sodium. Exchanges: 0 Grain (Starch); 7 Lean Meat; ½ Fat; ½ Other Carbohydrates.

LC SERVING SUGGESTIONS: Serve with Faux-tay-toe Salad (page 247) and Basic Coleslaw (page 255).

SERVING SUGGESTION: Slap the beef on whole-wheat hamburger buns.

# SUMMER

# ✳ Week One

**DAY ONE:** Tandoori-Style Chicken

**DAY TWO:** Thai Beef Salad

**DAY THREE:** Greek Turkey Burgers

**DAY FOUR:** Pub Pork Ribs

**DAY FIVE:** Skillet Salmon with Horseradish Cream

**DAY SIX:** Crock Swiss Steak

## SHOPPING LIST

### MEAT

4 boneless, skinless chicken breast halves

1 pound flank steak

1 pound round steak

1 pound ground turkey

1½ pounds pork spareribs

4 salmon fillets

### CONDIMENTS

olive oil

vegetable oil

teriyaki sauce

rice vinegar

vinegar (if not using beer)

peanut butter

barbecue sauce

low-fat mayonnaise; **lc extra

horseradish sauce

**lc salad dressing—your favorite

**PRODUCE**

3 pounds onions (keep on hand)

1 head garlic (you'll need 6 cloves)

1 piece gingerroot (you'll need 3 tablespoons)

1 head red cabbage

1 head green cabbage

1 head romaine lettuce

1 bunch cilantro (you'll need ¼ cup)

1 large cucumber (you'll need ¼ of it + ½)

1 tomato; **lc 3–4 extra

mint (you'll need 4 teaspoons)

**lc 1 head lettuce (*not* iceberg) (1 meal)

**lc 1 bag coleslaw mix (1 meal)

**lc fresh basil

**lc celery sticks (1 meal)

**lc 2 heads cauliflower (2 meals)

**lc eggplant (1 meal)

**lc yellow squash (1 meal)

**lc zucchini (1 meal)

**lc salad veggies (1 meal)

**red rose potatoes (1 meal)

**russet potatoes (1 meal)

**CANNED GOODS**

1 8-ounce can tomato sauce

**SPICES**

basil

cayenne pepper

curry powder

ginger

garlic powder

Italian seasoning

onion powder

red pepper flakes

sesame seeds

thyme

kosher salt—optional

**DAIRY/DAIRY CASE**

buttermilk (you'll need 1 cup + 1 tablespoon)

plain yogurt (you'll need ½ cup)

low-fat sour cream (you'll need ½ cup)

1 egg

Feta cheese (you'll need ½ cup)

**lc 2 8-ounce packages cream cheese

**potato salad (or make your own)

**DRY GOODS**

sugar (or Splenda)

brown sugar

**1–2 pounds brown rice (2 meals)

**angel hair pasta (about 2 ounces per person)

**BAKERY**

1 loaf low-carb whole-wheat bread (you'll need 1–2 slices)

**OTHER**

beer or beer substitute (you'll need 2 cups, if not using
   ginger ale)

ginger ale (you'll need 2 cups, if not using beer)

# TANDOORI-STYLE CHICKEN

*2 teaspoons curry powder*

*2 teaspoons ginger*

*1 teaspoon onion powder*

*1 teaspoon garlic powder*

*½ teaspoon cayenne pepper, or to taste*

*Salt and pepper to taste*

*1 tablespoon sugar*

*1 cup buttermilk*

*4 boneless, skinless chicken breast halves*

CUCUMBER SAUCE

*¼ cucumber, chopped*

*½ cup plain yogurt*

*1 teaspoon mint, chopped fine*

To make the chicken: In a large, zipper-topped plastic bag, place the spices and buttermilk and mix well. Add the chicken. Mush the chicken around to evenly coat. Leave in the fridge while you prepare the rest of the dinner.

To make the Cucumber Sauce: Mix together the cucumber, yogurt, and mint.

Preheat outside grill or grilling appliance, or if you are using the broiler, preheat the broiler to about medium-high heat.

Remove chicken from the marinade and discard leftover marinade. Place chicken on a clean grill and cook evenly on both sides, about 5 minutes per side, depending on the thickness of the chicken. Serve with Cucumber Sauce.

PER SERVING
200 Calories; 3g Fat (15.1% calories from fat); 31g Protein; 10g Carbohydrate; 1g Dietary Fiber; 74mg Cholesterol; 157mg Sodium. Exchanges: 0 Grain (Starch); 4 Lean Meat; 0 Vegetable; ½ Non-Fat Milk; ½ Fat; ½ Other Carbohydrates.

LC SERVING SUGGESTIONS: Grilled yellow squash and zucchini.

SERVING SUGGESTION: Serve with brown rice.

DO-AHEAD TIP: Marinate the beef for tomorrow night's dinner.

# THAI BEEF SALAD

3 tablespoons teriyaki sauce

2 tablespoons vegetable oil

3 tablespoons gingerroot, grated

6 cloves garlic, pressed

1 teaspoon red pepper flakes, or less

1 tablespoon rice vinegar

1 pound flank steak


2 cups shredded red cabbage

2 cups shredded green cabbage

2 cups romaine lettuce, shredded

¼ cup cilantro, chopped

1 tablespoon mint leaves, chopped

1 teaspoon sesame seeds

### THAI SALAD DRESSING

2 tablespoons teriyaki sauce

2 tablespoons peanut butter

1 teaspoon rice vinegar


In a large, zipper-topped plastic bag, throw the first six ingredients in and mix well. Add the flank steak and turn to coat well, several times. Preferably refrigerate overnight for at least 6 hours.

Preheat outside grill or grilling appliance, or if you are using the broiler, preheat the broiler to about medium-high heat. Cook beef to desired wellness. Cool before slicing.

In a large mixing bowl, add the cabbages and the romaine; toss together well. In a smaller mixing bowl, mix together ingredients for Thai Salad Dressing.

Add the cooled meat to the salad and toss all together with the dressing. Divvy up onto plates and top with cilantro first, then a little mint, and finally a pinch of sesame seeds. Serve.

PER SERVING

366 Calories; 23g Fat (56.0% calories from fat); 28g Protein; 13g Carbohydrate; 3g Dietary Fiber; 58mg Cholesterol; 997mg Sodium. Exchanges: 0 Grain (Starch); 3½ Lean Meat; 2 Vegetable; 2½ Fat; 0 Other Carbohydrates.

LC SERVING SUGGESTION: Serve with celery sticks.

SERVING SUGGESTION: Add chilled cooked angel hair pasta, about 2 ounces per person.

# GREEK TURKEY BURGERS

*Serves 4*

1 egg, *lightly beaten*
1 pound ground turkey
⅓ cup whole-wheat bread crumbs (*toast bread and crumble*)
1 tablespoon buttermilk
2 teaspoons Italian seasoning
1 teaspoon garlic powder
*Salt and pepper to taste*

### TOMATO FETA RELISH

1 tomato, diced
½ cucumber, diced
½ cup feta cheese, *crumbled*

In a mixing bowl, mix together the egg, turkey, bread crumbs, buttermilk, and seasonings. I use very *clean hands* to get it all mushed together. Form 4 patties, salt and pepper them to taste.

In another, smaller mixing bowl, mix together the tomato, cucumber, and Feta to make Tomato Feta Relish. Salt and pepper to taste and toss lightly. Refrigerate until needed.

Preheat outside grill or grilling appliance, or if you are using the broiler, preheat the broiler to about medium-high heat.

Grill turkey patties on both sides, about 5 minutes on a side. Turkey should be cooked through and not pink. Serve with Tomato Feta Relish on the top.

### PER SERVING

286 Calories; 15g Fat (48.3% calories from fat); 26g Protein; 11g Carbohydrate; 2g Dietary Fiber; 153mg Cholesterol; 412mg Sodium. Exchanges: ½ Grain (Starch); 3½ Lean Meat; ½ Vegetable; 0 Non-Fat Milk; 1 Fat.

LC SERVING SUGGESTIONS: Serve with grilled eggplant and onions and a big green salad.

SERVING SUGGESTION: Add red potatoes.

DO-AHEAD TIP: Brine your ribs overnight.

# PUB PORK RIBS

*Serves 4*

*2 cups beer or beer substitute (or ginger ale with 1 tablespoon of vinegar)*
*2 teaspoons salt, preferably kosher*
*2 tablespoons brown sugar*
*1½ pounds pork spareribs, cut into small 2-rib portions*
*3 tablespoons barbecue sauce*

In a large, zipper-topped plastic bag, add the beer, salt, brown sugar, and spare ribs. Mush around. Marinate for at least 8 hours, preferably overnight.

Remove the ribs from the bag and discard the brine.

Preheat outside grill or grilling appliance, or if you are using the broiler, preheat the broiler to about medium-high heat.

Place the ribs on the grill, cover, and cook for 1 hour or until pork is no longer pink. Turn as often as needed to prevent burning. Heat the barbecue sauce and brush half on the ribs in the last 5 minutes of grilling.

Serve ribs with remaining barbecue sauce brushed on just before serving.

**PER SERVING**
376 Calories; 25g Fat (66.2% calories from fat); 19g Protein; 10g Carbohydrate; trace Dietary Fiber; 82mg Cholesterol; 3381mg Sodium. Exchanges: 2½ Lean Meat; 3½ Fat; ½ Other Carbohydrates.

**LC SERVING SUGGESTIONS:** Basic Coleslaw (page 255) and Faux-tay-toe Salad (page 247).

**SERVING SUGGESTION:** Serve also with regular potato salad.

# SKILLET SALMON WITH
# HORSERADISH CREAM

*Serves 4*

1 tablespoon olive oil
4 salmon fillets
Salt and pepper to taste
½ teaspoon basil
½ teaspoon garlic powder

### HORSERADISH CREAM

½ cup low-fat sour cream
1 tablespoon low-fat mayonnaise
1 tablespoon horseradish sauce

To make the fillets: In a skillet, heat the olive oil. Season the fish with salt and pepper to taste, basil, and garlic powder on both sides. Cook fish in the skillet for 5 minutes each side till nicely browned and fish flakes easily when tested with a fork.

To make the Horseradish Cream: Meanwhile, in a small mixing bowl, combine sour cream, mayonnaise, and horseradish sauce.

Serve cooked fillets with a dollop of Horseradish Cream on top.

### PER SERVING

284 Calories; 13g Fat (41.4% calories from fat); 36g Protein; 4g Carbohydrate; trace Dietary Fiber; 98mg Cholesterol; 179mg Sodium. Exchanges: 0 Grain (Starch); 5 Lean Meat; 1½ Fat; ½ Other Carbohydrates.

LC SERVING SUGGESTION: Serve with Caprice Salad (page 256).

SERVING SUGGESTION: Add brown rice.

# CROCK SWISS STEAK

*1 tablespoon olive oil*
*1 pound round steak*
*Salt and pepper to taste*
*1 onion, sliced*
*½ teaspoon thyme*
*8 ounces tomato sauce*
*½ cup water*

In a skillet over medium-high heat, warm the olive oil. Add the steak first, searing well on one side, then searing again on the other. Season with salt and pepper to taste.

Place the meat in the bottom of a Crock-Pot. Now add the onion to the skillet and cook till slightly browned and beginning to turn translucent, about 2 minutes. Add onion to the top of the meat.

Again, season the top with salt and pepper to taste, and sprinkle the thyme evenly. Carefully pour the tomato sauce evenly over the top.

Back to the skillet for a minute. Add ½ cup of water to the skillet and heat on high. Using a wire whisk, scrape up the little bits off the bottom of the pan and allow the liquid to reduce by half. Add this, too, to the Crock-Pot. Now cover and cook 8 to 10 hours on low, depending on the type of slow cooker you have.

PER SERVING
274 Calories; 17g Fat (56.8% calories from fat); 23g Protein; 7g Carbohydrate; 1g Dietary Fiber; 67mg Cholesterol; 401mg Sodium. Exchanges: 0 Grain (Starch); 3 Lean Meat; 1 Vegetable; 1½ Fat.

LC SERVING SUGGESTIONS: Serve with Mashed Faux-tay-toes (page 246) and steamed broccoli.

SERVING SUGGESTION: Add real mashed potatoes.

## GETTING WHAT YOU WANT

 Occasionally, you might have difficulty getting an ingredient or two at the grocery store if you live in a smaller community: La Tortilla Factory tortillas, for example, or even flank steak. I've received e-mails from subscribers telling me they couldn't get cilantro in their stores, and they live in the United States. In California, cilantro is right next to the parsley and sells just as swiftly. But not everyone lives in California.

I try hard to ensure that I don't throw in any oddball ingredients requiring you to make special trips to gourmet markets or place Internet orders (with the exception being La Tortilla's tortillas). But there are always exceptions, and smaller markets in more rural areas may not carry exactly what you need. Don't be discouraged—there is a way to get this worked out.

Remember this: Competition is stiff for your grocery dollar. To get what you want, keep that in mind when you talk to the manager of the department where you are shopping (meat, produce, dairy, etc.) or the manager of the store. Telling the cashier or bagger what you need probably won't get you the results you want.

Politely talk to the manager and tell them that you spend _____ amount of dollars in that store every week and that you've been a loyal customer since Nixon was in office (or whatever pertains to your situation). You need cilantro to start being carried in the produce section. Can you count on him to start ordering it? If he hems and haws, take your business elsewhere. I promise you— there are markets out there that need and want your business and don't mind getting you what you need.

The bottom line is, don't just slink away. Tell them what you want, and if that doesn't work, find a store that will respond.

## ✳ Week Two

DAY ONE: Mu Shu Chicken
DAY TWO: BBQ Beef Kabobs
DAY THREE: Greek Summer Fish
DAY FOUR: Pork Chops and Squash
DAY FIVE: Taco Salad
DAY SIX: Red Stuffed Peppers

### SHOPPING LIST

#### MEAT
4 boneless, skinless chicken breast halves
1 pound ground chicken
1 pound extra-lean ground beef
1 pound sirloin steak
4 boneless pork chops, about ½ inch thick
4 fish fillets (cod or halibut is good)

#### CONDIMENTS
olive oil
vegetable oil
ketchup
low-sodium soy sauce
plum preserves (need 2 tablespoons)
balsamic vinegar
vinegar (if not using red wine)
Worcestershire sauce
Italian salad dressing—your favorite
**lc salad dressing—your favorite
**mayonnaise

## PRODUCE

3 pounds onions (keep on hand)

2 heads garlic (you'll need 13 cloves)

1 16-ounce bag shredded cabbage

1 10-ounce bag baby lettuce leaves

1 carrot

2 bunches green onions; **lc additional

1 bunch cilantro (you'll need ½ cup)

5 red bell peppers

2 yellow squash

2 zucchini

3 tomatoes

**lc 1 head lettuce (*not* iceberg) (1 meal)

**lc 1 head cauliflower (1 meal)

**lc 1 head broccoli (1 meal)

**lc 1 bag coleslaw mix (1 meal)

**lc 1 bag spinach (1 meal)

**lc asparagus (1 meal)

**lc green beans (1 meal)

**lc salad veggies (1 meal)

**red rose potatoes (1 meal)

## CANNED GOODS

1 14½-ounce can diced tomatoes

1 14½-ounce can chicken broth

## SPICES

basil

bay leaf

chili powder

cumin

cayenne pepper

garlic powder

red pepper flakes

oregano

**DAIRY/DAIRY CASE**

butter

low-fat sour cream (you'll need 2 tablespoons)

Feta cheese (you'll need 1 cup)

low-fat Cheddar cheese (you'll need 3 cups); **lc
    additional

**lc eggs (you'll need to hard-boil)

**lc 8-ounce package cream cheese

**DRY GOODS**

whole-wheat flour

**2–3 pounds brown rice (4 meals)

**BAKERY**

**lc low-carb whole-wheat tortillas (2 meals)

** flour or whole-wheat tortillas (for quesadillas)

**OTHER**

red wine (you'll need ½ cup, if not using red grape juice)

red grape juice (you'll need ½ cup, if not using red wine)

bamboo or metal skewers

# MU SHU CHICKEN

*Serves 4*

*1 tablespoon vegetable oil*
*3 cloves garlic, pressed*
*4 boneless, skinless chicken breast halves, cut into strips*
*16 ounces shredded cabbage*
*4 green onions, chopped and divided*
*1 carrot, grated*
*1 tablespoon ketchup*
*2 teaspoons plum preserves*
*2 tablespoons low-sodium soy sauce*
*½ teaspoon red pepper flakes, or to taste*

In a skillet or wok, heat the oil over medium-high heat. Add the garlic and start stir-frying. Now add the chicken. When the chicken is nearly done, add the cabbage (in batches, if necessary), half the green onions, and the carrot. Cook till all is tender.

Now add remaining ingredients, except the reserved green onions. Continue to stir-fry till sauce is cooked through and all is hot. Sprinkle the top with reserved green onions and serve.

**PER SERVING**
221 Calories; 5g Fat (21.2% calories from fat); 30g Protein; 14g Carbohydrate; 4g Dietary Fiber; 68mg Cholesterol; 453mg Sodium. Exchanges: 0 Grain (Starch); 4 Lean Meat; 2 Vegetable; ½ Fat; 0 Other Carbohydrates.

**LC SERVING SUGGESTION:** Serve like real restaurant Mu Shu, and use a warmed, low-carb flour tortilla to roll the Mu Shu mixture in. Add some sautéed green beans (see sidebar on page 251).

**SERVING SUGGESTION:** Serve with brown rice as well.

**DO-AHEAD TIP:** Marinate the beef for tomorrow night's dinner.

# BBQ BEEF KABOBS

*Serves 4*

1 small onion, minced
6 cloves garlic, pressed
½ cup red wine (or red grape juice with a splash of vinegar)
2 tablespoons olive oil
2 tablespoons balsamic vinegar
1 bay leaf
1 pound sirloin steak, trimmed, cut in 2-inch cubes
1 red bell pepper, cut in 1-inch pieces
1 onion, cut in 1-inch pieces
Bamboo or metal skewers

In a large, zipper-topped plastic bag, add the onion, garlic, wine, olive oil, vinegar, and bay leaf and mush all together. Now add the beef to this mixture and mush it up again. Allow to marinate in the fridge at least 4 hours, preferably overnight.

If using bamboo, soak the bamboo skewers in water for at least 30 minutes prior to barbecuing to prevent them from igniting. Preheat the grill.

Remove the beef from the bag and throw out the marinade, then throw out the bag (don't even *think* about recycling that nasty bag! Cootie Central!). Thread the beef onto the skewers, alternating with the veggies.

Place the kabobs on the grill and turn often to avoid burning the veggies, about 2 or 3 minutes on each side, cooking for a total of 8 to 15 minutes, depending on how rare you like your beef. Serve immediately.

**PER SERVING**
347 Calories; 23g Fat (61.8% calories from fat); 22g Protein; 9g Carbohydrate; 2g Dietary Fiber; 71mg Cholesterol; 80mg Sodium. Exchanges: 3 Lean Meat; 1½ Vegetable; 0 Fruit; 2½ Fat.

**LC SERVING SUGGESTION:** Serve with Faux-tay-toe Salad (page 247) and Basic Coleslaw (page 255).

**SERVING SUGGESTION:** Add some brown rice.

# GREEK SUMMER FISH

*Serves 4*

*2 tablespoons whole-wheat flour*
*Salt and pepper to taste*
*4 fish fillets (cod or halibut is good)*
*2 tablespoons olive oil, divided*
*1 onion, chopped*
*2 cloves garlic, pressed*
*1 14½-ounce can diced tomatoes*
*½ teaspoon oregano*
*⅛ teaspoon red pepper flakes*
*1 cup Feta cheese, crumbled*

On a dinner plate, place the flour and salt and pepper to taste. Dredge the fish.

In a skillet, over a medium-high heat, heat half the olive oil. Brown the fish well on both sides. Fish should be almost done. Remove from skillet and keep warm.

In the skillet, heat the remaining olive oil and add the onion and garlic. Cook the onion till nearly translucent and add the tomatoes (with the juice) and spices. Again add salt and pepper to taste. Bring to a boil; turn it down to simmer to reduce the sauce (about 5 to 10 minutes).

Serve fish with tomato sauce spooned over the top and crumbled Feta strewn over the top of the tomatoes.

**PER SERVING**
391 Calories; 17g Fat (38.5% calories from fat); 48g Protein; 11g Carbohydrate; 2g Dietary Fiber; 133mg Cholesterol; 691mg Sodium. Exchanges: 0 Grain (Starch); 6½ Lean Meat; 1 Vegetable; 2½ Fat.

**LC SERVING SUGGESTION:** Serve with steamed asparagus.

**SERVING SUGGESTION:** Add brown rice.

# PORK CHOPS AND SQUASH

*Serves 4*

*2 tablespoons whole-wheat flour*
*1 teaspoon garlic powder*
*Salt and pepper to taste*
*4 boneless pork chops, about ½ inch thick*
*2 tablespoons olive oil, divided*
*1 onion, chopped*
*2 yellow squash, sliced*
*2 zucchini, sliced*
*1 tomato, diced*
*1 teaspoon basil*
*1 cup chicken broth*
*1 tablespoon butter*

On a dinner plate, mix together the flour, garlic, and salt and pepper. Dredge the chops both sides in this mixture.

In a skillet, heat half the olive oil over medium-high heat. Add the pork and cook about 5 minutes each side or until cooked through. Remove from the skillet and keep warm.

Add the remaining oil to the skillet, and then add the onion, squashes, tomato, basil, and salt and pepper. Sauté till veggies are crisp-tender. Remove from pan and keep warm.

Add the chicken broth into the skillet and, with a wire whisk, whisk up the browned bits. Turn up the heat and allow the broth to reduce by about half. Add the butter now and whisk to blend.

Add the veggies and the pork chops back to the skillet and warm. When everything is nice and hot, place chop first on the plate, then some veggies, and finally spoon a little sauce over the top. Serve.

**PER SERVING**
304 Calories; 17g Fat (49.8% calories from fat); 26g Protein; 13g Carbohydrate; 4g Dietary Fiber; 74mg Cholesterol; 280mg Sodium. Exchanges: 0 Grain (Starch); 3 Lean Meat; 1½ Vegetable; 2 Fat.

**LC SERVING SUGGESTION:** Serve with a big green salad.

**SERVING SUGGESTION:** Add red potatoes.

# TACO SALAD

*Serves 4*

*1 pound ground chicken*

*Salt and pepper to taste*

*10 ounces baby lettuce leaves*

*2 tomatoes, chopped*

*2 tablespoons Italian salad dressing—your favorite*

*1 tablespoon Worcestershire sauce*

*1 teaspoon chili powder*

*1 teaspoon garlic powder*

*1 teaspoon cumin*

*½ teaspoon red pepper flakes*

*¼ teaspoon cayenne pepper*

*Salt and pepper to taste*

*4 green onions, chopped*

*½ cup cilantro, chopped*

*1½ cups shredded low-fat Cheddar cheese*

In a skillet, brown the meat, season with salt and pepper to taste, and set aside to cool.

Now, to a large salad bowl, add the lettuce. In a smaller bowl, add the tomatoes, dressing, and all the seasonings. Toss well to mix. Add the tomato mixture to the meat and mix well.

Add remaining ingredients to the salad bowl, including the meat mixture, and toss well. Then divvy up onto plates and serve.

PER SERVING
403 Calories; 18g Fat (39.6% calories from fat); 48g Protein; 13g Carbohydrate; 3g Dietary Fiber; 116mg Cholesterol; 485mg Sodium. Exchanges: 0 Grain (Starch); 6½ Lean Meat; 1 Vegetable; 0 Fruit; ½ Fat; 0 Other Carbohydrates.

LC SERVING SUGGESTION: Serve with quesadillas made with low-carb tortillas.

SERVING SUGGESTION: Use regular flour tortillas (whole wheat is better) for the quesadillas.

# RED STUFFED PEPPERS

*Serves 4*

*4 red bell peppers*
*1 onion, chopped*
*1 pound extra-lean ground beef*
*Salt and pepper to taste*
*½ teaspoon oregano*
*½ teaspoon basil*
*1 teaspoon garlic powder*
*1½ cups shredded low-fat Cheddar cheese*
*2 tablespoons sour cream*

Using a paring knife, remove the top of the peppers, trying to get only the stem and not too much pepper. Remove the ribs and seeds with your fingers. If necessary, lightly tap on a countertop cut side down to loosen seeds. Rinse pepper.

Heat a skillet over medium-high for about 2 or 3 minutes. You want it nice and hot. For this purpose, you should use a regular skillet, not a nonstick.

Now lay the red peppers on their sides and, as they start to smoke, move them around. Allow peppers to get tender and slightly blackened. You are dry-roasting them before stuffing them. Set aside and allow to cool.

In the same skillet, cook the onions and ground beef together; season with salt and pepper as you go. Drain well and blot with paper towels to get any extra grease. This will save you on fat grams, although it won't show up in the nutritional info.

Add the seasonings to the beef and 1 cup of shredded cheese. Mix well. Stuff the peppers with this mixture and place them in the Crock-Pot standing up. You might need something in the middle—like a dishwasher-proof coffee cup—to help keep them upright against the Crock-Pot walls.

Next, cook on low for 8 hours or so, depending on the type of slow cooker you have, or until peppers are nice and tender. At the last 15 minutes of cooking time, sprinkle the tops with the additional cheese. Serve with a dollop of sour cream.

**PER SERVING**

447 Calories; 25g Fat (54.7% calories from fat); 31g Protein; 12g Carbohydrate; 3g Dietary
Fiber; 109mg Cholesterol; 344mg Sodium. Exchanges: 0 Grain (Starch); 4 Lean Meat; 1½ Vegetable; 0 Non-Fat Milk; 5 Fat.

LC SERVING SUGGESTION: Serve with a big spinach salad.

SERVING SUGGESTION: Add brown rice.

## THE THRILL OF THE GRILL

✳ Who doesn't love the smoky, sexy flavor of meat grilled to juicy perfection over an outdoor grill? And listen, if you can get that from grilling your beef, how about those veggies? They're practically begging for the outdoor treatment.

One nifty tip I picked up for grilling asparagus was to make a "raft" out of the asparagus using pre-soaked bamboo skewers (soak them in water for 30 minutes before grilling to prevent them from igniting) and brushing the asparagus with a little olive oil beforehand. Let me tell you, asparagus on the grill is just a little slice of heaven.

When using a barbecue, whether it is gas or charcoal, it is imperative to preheat the grill. You cannot put the food on a cold grill and start that way for the same reasons you don't stick food in an oven that hasn't been preheated—it messes up the cooking time and the way it should cook. Don't rush this important preheat step.

There are some wonderful grilling accessories that I just cannot live without. You should try them, too. One is a hole-y wok. That's right . . . big holes in a flat-bottomed wok. I grilled the most incredible stir-fried squash in one of those things. It was easy—sliced zucchini, summer squash, and a little olive oil and garlic tossed together in the bowl got thrown into that wok and those vegetables were amazing. Think of the possibilities!

I also purchased a flat hole-y cookie-sheet-looking thing. That is how I cook my fish without losing it through the grill slats.

One last thing you need for the barby is a set of grilling tools. I used to use my kitchen spatula till the one day I burned the hair off my arm when I was turning chicken. That was enough to convince me.

Use real grilling tools and spend a few dollars on some nice ones. Lousy tools give you lousy results. Don't forget a good wire brush, too. Keeping the grill immaculate will improve what you're eating immensely. "Burning off" the old food works only to a degree—you need the brush!

# ✳ Week Three

DAY ONE: Turkey Pomodoro

DAY TWO: Teriyaki Fish

DAY THREE: Chicken with Dijon-Tarragon Sauce

DAY FOUR: Low-Carb Skillet Beef Stroganoff

DAY FIVE: Shrimp and Snow Peas

DAY SIX: Summer Crock

## SHOPPING LIST

### MEAT

4 boneless, skinless chicken breast halves

8 turkey breast cutlets

1 pound top sirloin

4 fish steaks (choose something meaty and firm such as
      tuna, shark, or swordfish)

1 pound large raw shrimp

1 pound Italian sausage

### CONDIMENTS

olive oil

vegetable oil

teriyaki sauce

Dijon mustard

vinegar (if not using white wine)

**lc salad dressing—your choice

**lc soy sauce

### PRODUCE

3 pounds onions (keep on hand)

1 head garlic (you'll need 5 cloves)

1–2 pieces gingerroot (you'll need 2 tablespoons)

mushrooms (you'll need 1½ cups)

eggplant (you'll need 1½ cups)

yellow squash (you'll need 1½ cups)

zucchini (you'll need 1½ cups)

1–2 lemons (you'll need 2 tablespoons juice)

1–2 tomatoes (you'll need ½ cup, diced)

1 bunch green onions

1 red bell pepper; **lc additional (1 meal)

1 pound snow peas

1 bag spinach (you'll need 4 cups)

**lc 3–4 heads lettuce (*not* iceberg) (4 meals)

**lc 1 bag baby greens (1 meal)

**lc 1 head red cabbage (1 meal)

**lc 1 head green cabbage (1 meal)

**lc salad veggies (4 meals)

**lc green beans (1 meal)

**lc asparagus (1 meal)

**lc zucchini (1 meal)

**red potatoes (2 meals)


## CANNED GOODS

2 14½-ounce cans chicken broth

1 14½-ounce can beef broth

1 14½-ounce can diced tomatoes


## SPICES

basil

cumin

garlic powder

paprika

red pepper flakes

tarragon

thyme

**DAIRY/DAIRY CASE**

butter

half-and-half (you'll need ⅓ cup)

sour cream (you'll need ½ cup)

**DRY GOODS**

whole-wheat flour

**1–2 pounds brown rice (2 meals)

**wide egg noodles (1 meal)

**BAKERY**

**whole-grain rolls

**OTHER**

white wine (you'll need ¼ cup + ½ cup, if not using
   chicken broth)

white grape juice (you'll need ¼ cup, if not using white
   wine)

# TURKEY POMODORO

*Serves 4*

This recipe traditionally deglazes the pan with vodka, but I use white wine. If you prefer, you can use all chicken broth.

> *2 tablespoons whole-wheat flour*
> *1 teaspoon garlic powder*
> *Salt and pepper to taste*
> *8 turkey breast cutlets*
> *1 tablespoon olive oil*
> *½ cup chicken broth*
> *½ cup white wine (or white grape juice with a splash of vinegar)*
> *2 tablespoons lemon juice*
> *½ cup tomatoes, diced*
> *½ teaspoon basil*
> *1 tablespoon butter*

On a dinner plate, mix together the flour, garlic powder, and salt and pepper. Dust cutlets in this mixture.

In a skillet, heat the olive oil over medium-high heat. Sauté the cutlets in the skillet till lightly browned on both sides. Remove from the pan and keep warm.

To the pan, add chicken broth and wine. Using a wire whisk, whisk up the bits off the bottom of the pan. Add the remaining ingredients, except the butter. Bring to simmer and let reduce somewhat to thicken. When the sauce is nearly finished, add the butter and incorporate into the sauce. Add back the cutlets and allow to warm completely. Now serve with sauce over the top.

PER SERVING
257 Calories; 8g Fat (32.0% calories from fat); 35g Protein; 5g Carbohydrate; 1g Dietary Fiber; 98mg Cholesterol; 353mg Sodium. Exchanges: 0 Grain (Starch); 5 Lean Meat; 0 Vegetable; 0 Fruit; 1½ Fat.

LC SERVING SUGGESTIONS: Sautéed green beans (see sidebar on page 251) and a big salad.

SERVING SUGGESTION: Add some red potatoes.

# TERIYAKI FISH

*½ cup teriyaki sauce*
*2 teaspoons gingerroot, grated*
*4 fish steaks (choose something meaty and firm such as tuna, shark, or swordfish)*

Place the teriyaki sauce and ginger in a large, zipper-topped plastic bag.

Add the steaks and marinate for about 30 minutes (less is okay, too). Prepare the rest of the meal.

Preheat outside grill or grilling appliance, or if you are using the broiler, preheat the broiler to about medium-high heat. Place the fish on the grill and turn after about 3 minutes or so, depending on its thickness. Fish is done if it flakes when tested with a fork (although meatier fish don't flake as much, it is still the right way to test for doneness).

**PER SERVING**
170 Calories; 1g Fat (6.3% calories from fat); 32g Protein; 6g Carbohydrate; trace Dietary Fiber; 73mg Cholesterol; 1472mg Sodium. Exchanges: 4 Lean Meat; 1 Vegetable.

**LC SERVING SUGGESTION:** Serve with grilled veggies: bell pepper, zucchini, and some onion.

**SERVING SUGGESTION:** Add brown rice.

210 ❄ SAVING DINNER THE LOW-CARB WAY

# CHICKEN WITH DIJON-
# TARRAGON SAUCE

*Serves 4*

*1 tablespoon olive oil, divided*
*1 tablespoon butter, divided*
*4 boneless, skinless chicken breast halves*
*Salt and pepper to taste*
*1 small onion, diced fine*
*¾ cup chicken broth*
*¼ cup white wine*
*⅓ cup half-and-half*
*1 teaspoon tarragon*
*2 teaspoons Dijon mustard*

In a skillet, melt half of each of the butter and olive oil together over medium-high heat. Season the chicken breasts with salt and pepper to taste. Cook till nicely browned on both sides, about 5 minutes per side, depending on the thickness. Remove from skillet and keep warm.

Add remaining butter and olive oil, then add the onion. Cook over medium heat till nicely soft, about 3 minutes. Add the chicken broth and simmer until it is has reduced. Use your wire whisk to get up all the browned bits off the bottom of the pan. Now add the wine. Cook for another 2 minutes and reduce the heat.

Add the half-and-half, tarragon, and Dijon into the skillet. Increase the heat, but don't boil it hard or the sauce will break. Allow to cook till thickened slightly; add the chicken back into the pan (and any juices that may have collected) and cook for a few more minutes.

Now serve with sauce ladled over the top.

**PER SERVING**
242 Calories; 10g Fat (41.5% calories from fat); 29g Protein; 4g Carbohydrate; 1g Dietary Fiber; 84mg Cholesterol; 290mg Sodium. Exchanges: 0 Grain (Starch); 4 Lean Meat; ½ Vegetable; 0 Non-Fat Milk; 1½ Fat; 0 Other Carbohydrates.

**LC SERVING SUGGESTIONS:** Serve with a heap of gorgeous, steamed asparagus and a lovely baby-greens salad. This is company food!

**SERVING SUGGESTION:** Add some red potatoes.

# LOW-CARB SKILLET
# BEEF STROGANOFF

*Serves 4*

1 tablespoon olive oil
1 onion, chopped
1½ cups mushrooms, sliced
1 pound top sirloin, sliced thinly
Salt and pepper to taste
2 tablespoons whole-wheat flour
1 cup beef broth
½ teaspoon thyme
½ cup sour cream
4 cups fresh spinach
1 teaspoon paprika

In a skillet over medium-high heat, heat the olive oil and sauté the onions for about 3 minutes. Add the mushrooms and keep cooking till the mushrooms begin to lose their liquid. Remove and keep warm. Add the beef and cook till completely browned; season with salt and pepper to taste as you go.

Drain the fat, if any, and sprinkle the flour over the top of the beef. Add the broth and cook until slightly thickened.

Add back the mushroom mixture and mix well. Season again with salt and pepper and add the thyme. Once hot, turn down the heat and add the sour cream. Don't let it boil, or the sour cream will turn into nasty little curds like cottage cheese; you don't want that.

Place 1 cup of raw spinach on each plate and top with the stroganoff. The heat from the stroganoff will wilt it nicely. You can sauté the spinach first if you like, but it's good this way. Sprinkle the top with paprika.

**PER SERVING**
370 Calories; 26g Fat (64.4% calories from fat); 26g Protein; 7g Carbohydrate; 2g Dietary Fiber; 78mg Cholesterol; 420mg Sodium. Exchanges: 0 Grain (Starch); 3½ Lean Meat; ½ Vegetable; 3½ Fat.

**LC SERVING SUGGESTION:** Just add a big salad.

**SERVING SUGGESTION:** Instead of serving it on spinach, serve traditionally on wide noodles.

# SHRIMP AND SNOW PEAS

*Serves 4*

*1 pound raw large shrimp, peeled and deveined*
*2 tablespoons vegetable oil, divided*
*2 cloves garlic, divided*
*4 teaspoons gingerroot, grated and divided*
*Salt and pepper to taste*
*¼ teaspoon red pepper flakes*
*1 pound snow peas, stringed*
*½ cup red bell pepper, chopped*
*3 green onions, chopped*

In a plastic bag, place the shrimp, half the oil, garlic, ginger, salt and pepper to taste, and the red pepper flakes. Place in the fridge while you prepare the rest of the meal (string the snow peas, make the salad, etc.).

Heat a wok or skillet over medium-high heat. Add the shrimp mixture and sauté quickly for about two minutes, or until shrimp are pink. Remove from skillet and keep warm.

To the skillet, add the remaining oil, ginger, and garlic, along with the veggies, cooking till veggies are crisp-tender, about 2 to 3 minutes. Add the shrimp and any cooking juices back in, and stir-fry for another minute or so to heat through. Serve.

**PER SERVING**
240 Calories; 9g Fat (34.2% calories from fat); 27g Protein; 12g Carbohydrate; 4g Dietary Fiber; 173mg Cholesterol; 175mg Sodium. Exchanges: 0 Grain (Starch); 3 Lean Meat; 2 Vegetable; 1½ Fat.

**LC SERVING SUGGESTIONS:** Serve on a bed of braised cabbage (see sidebar on page 254), with a splash of soy sauce on the top. Add a green salad and you're set.

**SERVING SUGGESTION:** Serve on a bed of brown rice instead.

# SUMMER CROCK

*Serves 4*

*1 pound Italian sausage, with casings removed*
*1 tablespoon olive oil*
*1 onion, chopped*
*1½ cups eggplant, cubed*
*1½ cups yellow squash, chopped*
*1½ cups zucchini, chopped*
*3 cloves garlic, pressed*
*¾ cup chicken broth*
*14½ ounces diced tomatoes, canned*
*2 teaspoons cumin*
*¼ teaspoon red pepper flakes*
*Salt and pepper to taste*

In a skillet, cook the sausage and, using a wooden spoon, crumble it. Drain grease and place the sausage in the Crock-Pot.

Add the olive oil to the skillet and heat over medium-high heat. Now add the onion, eggplant, squashes, and garlic, sautéing about 2 minutes. Add this to the Crock-Pot.

Now add the broth to the skillet and bring to a boil. Using a wire whisk, get all the stuff up off the bottom of the skillet and incorporate into the broth. Allow to boil vigorously for about a minute. Pour this over the top of the Crock-Pot.

One last time in the skillet, add the tomatoes and their juice and the seasonings. Heat to a boil, then add on top of everything else in the Crock-Pot. Cover and cook on low for 6 to 8 hours, depending on the type of slow cooker you have, or till veggies are tender but not over-cooked.

**PER SERVING**
469 Calories; 20g Fat (32.4% calories from fat); 20g Protein; 14g Carbohydrate; 4g Dietary Fiber; 86mg Cholesterol; 988mg Sodium. Exchanges: 0 Grain (Starch); 2½ Lean Meat; 2½ Vegetable; 6½ Fat.

**LC SERVING SUGGESTION:** A big green salad.

**SERVING SUGGESTION:** Add whole-grain rolls.

## ✳ Week Four

DAY ONE: Skillet Chicken with Honey-Mustard Mayo

DAY TWO: Mega-Layered Chef Salad

DAY THREE: Grilled Ginger Salmon

DAY FOUR: Seared Turkey on Spinach

DAY FIVE: Orange-Glazed Beef

DAY SIX: Crock Chops

### SHOPPING LIST

**MEAT**

4 boneless, skinless chicken breast halves

1 pound beef sirloin

4 pork chops, about ½ inch thick

4 salmon fillets

1 cup turkey ham

8 turkey breast cutlets

1 cup boneless, skinless turkey breast, cooked

**CONDIMENTS**

olive oil

Dijon mustard

honey

ketchup

teriyaki sauce

low-fat mayonnaise; **lc additional

vinegar (if not using white wine)

balsamic vinegar

**PRODUCE**

3 pounds onions (keep on hand)

1 piece gingerroot (you'll need 4 teaspoons)

1 head romaine lettuce

1 bag spinach (you'll need 4 cups)

1 bunch green onions (you'll need ½ cup); **additional

1 bunch Italian parsley (you'll need 1 tablespoon)

celery (you'll need ½ cup)

2 red bell peppers

1–2 oranges (you'll need ¼ cup juice, if not buying frozen
or in carton)

**lc 2–3 heads lettuce (*not* iceberg) (3 meals)

**lc 1 bag coleslaw mix (1 meal)

**lc broccoli (2 meals)

**lc 2 heads cauliflower (2 meals)

**lc asparagus

**lc salad veggies (3 meals)

**russet potatoes (1 meal)

**red potatoes

## CANNED GOODS

1 jar capers (you'll need 2 tablespoons)

## SPICES

cayenne pepper

cumin

curry powder

garlic powder

marjoram

thyme

## DAIRY/DAIRY CASE

2 eggs (you'll need to hard-boil); **lc additional (also hard-
boiled)

Romano cheese (you'll need 1 tablespoon)

orange juice (you'll need ¼ cup, if not using fresh squeezed
or frozen)

**lc 2 8-ounce packages cream cheese

### DRY GOODS
brown sugar

whole-wheat flour

**1–2 pounds brown rice (2 meals)

### FROZEN FOODS
orange juice (you'll need ¼ cup, if not using fresh squeezed
or in carton)

### BAKERY
**whole-grain rolls

### OTHER
white wine (you'll need ½ cup, if not using white grape
juice)

white grape juice (you'll need ½ cup, if not using white
wine)

# SKILLET CHICKEN WITH HONEY-MUSTARD MAYO

*Serves 4*

4 boneless, skinless chicken breast halves
Salt and pepper to taste
½ teaspoon garlic powder
¼ teaspoon thyme
⅛ teaspoon cayenne pepper
1 tablespoon olive oil

HONEY-MUSTARD MAYO

¼ cup low-fat mayonnaise
1½ tablespoons honey
2 tablespoons Dijon mustard

To make the chicken: On a dinner plate, season the chicken breasts on both sides with the seasonings.

In a skillet, heat the olive oil over medium-high heat and sauté chicken, browning well for about 5 minutes each side, or until chicken is cooked through.

To make the Honey-Mustard Mayo: In a small bowl whisk together all the ingredients.

Serve each cooked breast with a dollop of the mayo sauce on top.

PER SERVING
231 Calories; 9g Fat (36.6% calories from fat); 28g Protein; 8g Carbohydrate; trace Dietary Fiber; 73mg Cholesterol; 242mg Sodium. Exchanges: 0 Grain (Starch); 4 Lean Meat; 1½ Fat; ½ Other Carbohydrates.

LC SERVING SUGGESTIONS: Serve with steamed broccoli and a big green salad.

SERVING SUGGESTION: Add steamed red potatoes.

DO-AHEAD TIP: To save yourself some time tomorrow, feel free to chop, chop, chop, then bag up some of those salad ingredients. Also, hard-boil the eggs if you haven't done so already.

# MEGA-LAYERED CHEF SALAD

*Serves 4*

*1 head romaine lettuce, chopped*
*½ cup celery, chopped*
*½ cup red bell pepper, chopped*
*½ cup green onions, chopped*
*2 eggs, hard-boiled, peeled, and quartered*
*1 cup turkey ham, chopped*
*1 cup boneless, skinless turkey breast, chopped*
*2 tablespoons Romano cheese, grated*

**DRESSING**

*1 cup low-fat mayonnaise*
*½ teaspoon garlic powder*
*½ teaspoon curry powder*
*1 tablespoon brown sugar*

In a 13- × 9-inch baking dish, layer half of the romaine lettuce. Follow with a layer of celery, bell pepper, green onion, and egg, and then a layer of ham and turkey. Follow that with the remaining romaine.

In a small bowl, whisk together the dressing ingredients. Now spread this mixture evenly over the top of the salad and sprinkle with the Romano cheese. Carefully cover and refrigerate until ready to serve.

**PER SERVING**
397 Calories; 23g Fat (52.3% calories from fat); 33g Protein; 14g Carbohydrate; 4g Dietary Fiber; 187mg Cholesterol; 1002mg Sodium. Exchanges: 0 Grain (Starch); 4 Lean Meat; 1½ Vegetable; 3½ Fat; ½ Other Carbohydrates.

**LC SERVING SUGGESTION:** You don't need a thing! Enjoy the salad.

**SERVING SUGGESTION:** Serve with whole-grain rolls.

# GRILLED GINGER SALMON

*Serves 4*

*4 teaspoons gingerroot, grated*
*4 teaspoons teriyaki sauce*
*4 salmon fillets*

Rub 1 teaspoon of gingerroot and 1 teaspoon teriyaki sauce on each fillet and place on a dinner plate, wrap with plastic, and let sit in the fridge while you get the rest of dinner ready.

Preheat outside grill or grilling appliance, or if you are using the broiler, preheat the broiler to about medium-high heat. Place the fish on the grill and turn after about 3 minutes or so, depending on the thickness of the fish. Fish is done if it flakes when tested with a fork.

PER SERVING
204 Calories; 6g Fat (27.1% calories from fat); 34g Protein; 1g Carbohydrate; trace Dietary Fiber; 88mg Cholesterol; 344mg Sodium. Exchanges: 5 Lean Meat; ½ Vegetable.

LC SERVING SUGGESTIONS: Serve with grilled asparagus and salad.

SERVING SUGGESTION: Serve with brown rice.

# SEARED TURKEY ON SPINACH

*2 tablespoons whole-wheat flour*
*Salt and pepper to taste*
*½ teaspoon marjoram*
*7 turkey breast cutlets*
*1 tablespoon olive oil*
*½ cup white wine*
*1 tablespoon balsamic vinegar*
*1 tablespoon Italian parsley, chopped fine*
*4 cups spinach, slightly damp*

On a dinner plate, sprinkle the flour, salt and pepper to taste, and marjoram; mix well. Place the turkey cutlets in the flour mixture and lightly dredge.

In a skillet, heat the olive oil over medium-high heat. Add the turkey and cook about 2 to 3 minutes on each side, till nicely browned. Remove from the pan and keep warm.

To the skillet, add the wine and vinegar and cook about 2 to 3 minutes, allowing the mixture to reduce and thicken. Add the turkey back in and warm for a minute. Remove from the heat.

Using another skillet (nonstick is preferable) heat the pan for just a minute over medium-high heat. Add the damp spinach and allow it to wilt just slightly, turning it quickly. Divvy up the spinach evenly and serve with the turkey and sauce on top. Sprinkle with the parsley, and serve.

### PER SERVING
224 Calories; 5g Fat (24.5% calories from fat); 35g Protein; 3g Carbohydrate; 1g Dietary Fiber; 90mg Cholesterol; 322mg Sodium. Exchanges: 0 Grain (Starch); 5 Lean Meat; 0 Vegetable; 0 Fruit; ½ Fat.

LC SERVING SUGGESTION: Serve with a big green salad, too.

SERVING SUGGESTION: Serve with brown rice.

# ORANGE-GLAZED BEEF

*Serves 4*

1 tablespoon whole-wheat flour
2 tablespoons brown sugar, divided
Salt and pepper to taste
½ teaspoon cumin
⅛ teaspoon cayenne pepper
1 pound beef sirloin, cut into strips
¼ cup orange juice
3 tablespoons balsamic vinegar
2 tablespoons capers
1 tablespoon olive oil

On a dinner plate, combine the flour, half the sugar, salt and pepper, cumin, and cayenne. Mix well and dredge beef in it.

In a small bowl, combine the remaining sugar, orange juice, vinegar, and capers. Stir well and make sure the sugar is completely dissolved.

In a skillet over medium-high heat, heat the olive oil. Add the beef strips, cooking about 2 minutes on each side. You want them nicely browned. Keep turning till well browned all over.

Add the vinegar mixture to the skillet with the beef, mixing well. Cook another minute until sauce thickens up, then serve.

**PER SERVING**
298 Calories; 20g Fat (60.2% calories from fat); 21g Protein; 8g Carbohydrate; trace Dietary Fiber; 72mg Cholesterol; 98mg Sodium. Exchanges: 0 Grain (Starch); 3 Lean Meat; 0 Fruit; 2 Fat; ½ Other Carbohydrates.

**LC SERVING SUGGESTIONS:** Serve with Mashed Faux-tay-toes (page 246) and steamed broccoli.

**SERVING SUGGESTION:** Add real mashed potatoes.

# CROCK CHOPS

*1 tablespoon olive oil*
*4 pork chops, about ½ inch thick*
*Salt and pepper to taste*
*1 onion, chopped*
*1 bell pepper, chopped*
*2 tablespoons ketchup*
*2 tablespoons brown sugar*

In a skillet, heat the olive oil. Brown the chops on both sides, seasoning with salt and pepper as you go. Set aside.

Now sauté the onion and bell pepper together for 1 or 2 minutes till wilted. Place at the bottom of a Crock-Pot. Place the browned pork chops on top of that.

In a small bowl, mix the ketchup and brown sugar, smear over the top of the chops. Cover and cook 7 to 9 hours on low, depending on the type of slow cooker you have.

**PER SERVING**
305 Calories; 18g Fat (54.3% calories from fat); 24g Protein; 11g Carbohydrate; 1g Dietary Fiber; 74mg Cholesterol; 151mg Sodium. Exchanges: 3½ Lean Meat; ½ Vegetable; 1½ Fat; ½ Other Carbohydrates.

**LC SERVING SUGGESTIONS:** Serve with Faux-tay-toe Salad (page 247) and Basic Coleslaw (page 255).

**SERVING SUGGESTION:** Add red potatoes.

# ✳ Week Five

DAY ONE: Spice-Rubbed Chicken

DAY TWO: Seared Pan Steaks with Red Wine Sauce

DAY THREE: Spinach Chicken Salad

DAY FOUR: Salmon Burgers with Dill Sauce

DAY FIVE: Hot-and-Spicy Pork Chops with Citrus Sauce

DAY SIX: French Country Crock Roast

## SHOPPING LIST

### MEAT

8 boneless, skinless chicken breast halves

4 petite steaks, lean, about 4 ounces each—your choice

2 pounds beef roast

8 pieces turkey bacon

4 pork chops, ½ inch thick

1 pound salmon (if not using canned)

### CONDIMENTS

olive oil

vegetable oil

vinegar (if not using red wine)

honey mustard salad dressing (you'll need 4 tablespoons)

**lc salad dressing—your favorite

### PRODUCE

3 pounds onions (keep on hand)

1 small red onion

2–3 heads garlic

1 bunch cilantro (you'll need about ⅔ cup)

fresh dill (you'll need 2 tablespoons)

1 bunch green onions

4 cherry tomatoes

3–4 lemons (you'll need ¼ cup + 1 tablespoon juice)

1–2 limes (you'll need 2 tablespoons juice)

1–2 oranges (you'll need ⅓ cup juice, if not buying frozen or in carton)

1 head romaine lettuce

1 bag spinach (you'll need 4 cups)

**lc 3–4 heads lettuce (*not* iceberg) (4 meals)

**lc green beans (1 meal)

**lc snow peas (1 meal)

**lc mushrooms (1 meal)

**lc zucchini (1 meal)

**lc 1 head cauliflower (1 meal)

**lc broccoli (2 meals)

**lc yellow squash (1 meal)

**lc salad veggies (4 meals)

**red potatoes (1 meal)

**russet potatoes (1 meal)

## CANNED GOODS

1 6-ounce can tomato paste (you'll need 2 teaspoons)

1 14½-ounce can beef broth

1 14½-ounce can chicken broth

1 16-ounce can salmon (if not using fresh)

## SPICES

black pepper

cumin

garlic powder

ground coriander

marjoram

red pepper flakes

rosemary

thyme

**DAIRY/DAIRY CASE**

butter

2 8-ounce packages cream cheese

half-and-half (you'll need ¼ cup)

3 eggs (you'll need to hard-boil 2 eggs)

orange juice (you'll need ⅓ cup, if not using fresh squeezed
  or frozen)

**lc low-fat Cheddar cheese

**DRY GOODS**

**lc 1–2 pounds brown rice (3 meals)

**FROZEN FOODS**

orange juice (you'll need ⅓ cup, if not using fresh squeezed
  or in carton)

**BAKERY**

**lc low-carb whole-wheat tortillas (1 meal)

**whole-grain rolls

**OTHER**

red wine (you'll need 1 cup, if not using red grape juice)

red grape juice (you'll need 1 cup, if not using red wine)

# SPICE-RUBBED CHICKEN

*Serves 4*

*8 cloves garlic, pressed*
*½ tablespoon black pepper*
*½ tablespoon ground coriander*
*⅓ cup cilantro, finely chopped*
*2 tablespoons lime juice*
*1 tablespoon vegetable oil*
*4 boneless, skinless chicken breast halves*

In a small bowl, thoroughly mix all ingredients, minus the chicken. Rub half of this all over the chicken on one side. Place chicken and remaining rub in the fridge while you get the rest of dinner ready.

Preheat the grill.

Place chicken rub side down and begin to cook, rotating if necessary to keep from burning, but don't flip it onto its other side. Once the chicken is cooking, use a barbecue brush to spread remaining rub to the top of the chicken. Cook about 5 minutes on each side.

PER SERVING
182 Calories; 5g Fat (25.9% calories from fat); 28g Protein; 5g Carbohydrate; 1g Dietary Fiber; 68mg Cholesterol; 83mg Sodium. Exchanges: 0 Grain (Starch); 4 Lean Meat; ½ Vegetable; 0 Fruit; ½ Fat.

LC SERVING SUGGESTIONS: Serve with grilled zucchini and yellow squash, and a big green salad.

SERVING SUGGESTION: Serve with brown rice as well.

DO-AHEAD TIP: Make the chicken for the Spinach Chicken Salad (Day 3, page 230) at the same time, grilled simply with salt and pepper and a touch of garlic powder.

# SEARED PAN STEAKS WITH RED WINE SAUCE

*Serves 4*

*4 petite steaks, lean, about 4 ounces each—your choice*
*1 tablespoon olive oil*
*½ onion, diced fine*
*2 cloves garlic, pressed*
*2 teaspoons tomato paste*
*½ cup red wine (or red grape juice with a splash of vinegar)*
*¾ cup beef broth*
*½ teaspoon thyme*

Heat the skillet or pan over medium-high heat (don't use a nonstick skillet) for about 2 minutes, till nice and hot. Add the steaks and cook for about 3 to 4 minutes per side, depending on how you like your steaks ultimately cooked (you may need to turn on the hood fan). Remove steaks and keep warm. Remember, they will keep cooking as they stay warm.

Add the oil to the pan. Then add the onion and garlic and, using a wire whisk, move the onion, garlic, and oil around, picking up the browned bits off the bottom of the pan. Let the onion and garlic soften and brown slightly.

To this mixture, add the tomato paste, red wine, beef broth, and thyme. Continue to whisk and turn the heat to high. Allow sauce to reduce for about 5 minutes, then add the steaks back to the pan for just a minute to warm, turning over to coat.

Now serve the steaks on plates with sauce poured over the top.

**PER SERVING**
353 Calories; 26g Fat (71.5% calories from fat); 20g Protein; 3g Carbohydrate; trace Dietary Fiber; 70mg Cholesterol; 329mg Sodium. Exchanges: 0 Grain (Starch); 2½ Lean Meat; ½ Vegetable; 3½ Fat.

**LC SERVING SUGGESTIONS:** Serve with sautéed green beans (see sidebar on page 251) and mushrooms, add a clove of pressed garlic, a dab of butter, and salt and pepper to taste. Throw a big salad onto the table, too.

**SERVING SUGGESTION:** Serve with herbed red potatoes.

# SPINACH CHICKEN SALAD

4 cups romaine lettuce, chopped
4 cups spinach
4 boneless, skinless chicken breast halves, cooked and chopped
2 eggs, hard-boiled, peeled, and quartered
4 pieces turkey bacon, cooked and chopped
4 cherry tomatoes, halved
4 green onions, chopped
4 tablespoons honey mustard salad dressing

On four dinner plates, divvy up the romaine first and make a bed. Add the spinach to the lettuce. Now top the spinach with the chicken, eggs, bacon, tomatoes, and green onions, spread evenly over the top of each salad. Top each salad with a tablespoon of dressing, and serve.

PER SERVING
275 Calories; 10g Fat (32.3% calories from fat); 35g Protein; 12g Carbohydrate; 2g Dietary Fiber; 187mg Cholesterol; 413mg Sodium. Exchanges: 4½ Lean Meat; 1 Vegetable; 1 Fat; ½ Other Carbohydrates.

LC SERVING SUGGESTION: Serve with quesadillas if you need more food, using low-carb tortillas, or skip it if the salad is enough.

SERVING SUGGESTION: Add whole-grain rolls.

# SALMON BURGERS WITH DILL SAUCE

*Serves 4*

*16 ounces salmon, flaked (you can use canned or fresh, already cooked)*

*¼ cup red onion, minced*

*1 tablespoon fresh dill, minced*

*1 egg, slightly beaten*

*1 tablespoon lemon juice*

*½ tablespoon olive oil*

DILL SAUCE

*¼ cup cream cheese*

*¼ cup half-and-half*

*1 tablespoon fresh dill, minced*

*Salt and pepper to taste*

To make the burgers: In a bowl, combine all burger ingredients (except the olive oil) and mix well together. Form into 4 patties, about 4 inches. Place in the fridge.

To make Dill Sauce: In a small saucepan, cook together the cream cheese and half-and-half, stirring as you go to prevent it from burning. Once completely smooth, allow to cool. Just before using, stir in the dill and salt and pepper to taste.

Now heat the olive oil in a skillet over medium-high heat. Carefully add the patties and cook till nicely browned on one side, about 5 minutes. Very carefully, turn the patties (they will fall apart easily if you're not careful) and brown again on the other side. Serve warm with Dill Sauce over the top.

PER SERVING
238 Calories; 14g Fat (52.0% calories from fat); 26g Protein; 2g Carbohydrate; trace Dietary Fiber; 127mg Cholesterol; 139mg Sodium. Exchanges: 3½ Lean Meat; 0 Vegetable; 0 Fruit; 0 Non-Fat Milk; 1½ Fat.

LC SERVING SUGGESTIONS: Serve with steamed broccoli and a green salad.

SERVING SUGGESTION: Add brown rice.

# HOT-AND-SPICY PORK CHOPS WITH CITRUS SAUCE

*Serves 4*

*4 pork chops, about ½ inch thick*
*1 teaspoon cumin*
*1 teaspoon garlic powder*
*2 tablespoons olive oil, divided*
*2 cloves garlic, pressed*
*⅓ cup orange juice*
*⅓ cup chicken broth*
*¼ cup lemon juice*
*¼ teaspoon red pepper flakes, or more if needed*
*1 tablespoon butter*
*¼ cup chopped cilantro*

Sprinkle both sides of chops with cumin and garlic powder.

In a skillet, heat the olive oil over medium-high heat. Add the chops and brown thoroughly on both sides, about 5 minutes per side. You want it to brown, not burn; check it to make sure it is cooking right. Remove chops from the skillet and keep warm.

Into the skillet, add the remaining olive oil and garlic. Cook another minute, careful not to burn the garlic. Now add the orange juice, broth, and lemon juice. Using a wire whisk, get all the browned bits up off the bottom of the skillet and allow the sauce to come to a boil. Turn it down and let it simmer about 4 minutes or until reduced. Add the red pepper flakes and butter, and stir till butter is melted. Now add the pork back in (plus any accumulated cooking juices) and allow to warm up. Serve chops with sauce spooned over the top and cilantro sprinkled on top of that.

**PER SERVING**
340 Calories; 25g Fat (65.7% calories from fat); 24g Protein; 5g Carbohydrate; trace Dietary Fiber; 81mg Cholesterol; 154mg Sodium. Exchanges: 0 Grain (Starch); 3½ Lean Meat; 0 Vegetable; ½ Fruit; 3 Fat.

**LC SERVING SUGGESTIONS:** Serve with sautéed snow peas and a big green salad.

**SERVING SUGGESTION:** Add brown rice.

# FRENCH COUNTRY CROCK ROAST

*Serves 4*

1 tablespoon olive oil
2 pounds beef roast
1 onion, chopped
4 cloves garlic, pressed
4 pieces turkey bacon, chopped
½ cup red wine (or red grape juice with a splash of vinegar)
½ teaspoon rosemary, crushed
½ teaspoon thyme
½ teaspoon marjoram
Salt and pepper to taste

In a large skillet or Dutch oven, heat the olive oil. Brown the roast on all sides and place in the Crock-Pot.

Now add the onion, garlic, and bacon and cook for a few minutes. Pour this over the top of the roast.

Add to the Crock-Pot the wine, seasonings, and salt and pepper to taste; cover and cook on low for about 8 to 10 hours, depending on the type of slow cooker you have.

**PER SERVING**
485 Calories; 30g Fat (58.6% calories from fat); 44g Protein; 4g Carbohydrate; 1g Dietary Fiber; 144mg Cholesterol; 319mg Sodium. Exchanges: 0 Grain (Starch); 5½ Lean Meat; ½ Vegetable; 5 Fat.

**LC SERVING SUGGESTIONS:** Mashed Faux-tay-toes (page 246) and steamed broccoli.

**SERVING SUGGESTION:** Add regular mashed potatoes.

## ✳ Week Six

**DAY ONE:** Barbecued Lemon Chicken
**DAY TWO:** Cobb Salad
**DAY THREE:** Unshished Kabobs
**DAY FOUR:** Wahoo Tacos
**DAY FIVE:** Ratatouille Turkey
**DAY SIX:** Crock Loaf

### SHOPPING LIST

**MEAT**

7 boneless, skinless chicken breast halves
4 slices turkey bacon
8 turkey breast cutlets
1½ pounds ground turkey
1 pound sirloin steak
4 fish fillets, cooked

**CONDIMENTS**

olive oil
vegetable oil
teriyaki sauce
rice vinegar
sesame oil
ketchup
vinaigrette dressing, homemade or bottled—your choice

**PRODUCE**

3 pounds onions (keep on hand)
1 small red onion
1 head garlic (you'll need 8 cloves)
1 bunch cilantro (you'll need 1 cup)

2–3 lemons (you'll need ½ cup juice)

3–4 limes (garnish + juice)

2 tomatoes; **lc additional (1 meal)

1 red pepper

3 green peppers

1 stalk celery

1 eggplant

1 zucchini

chilies (garnish)

2 avocados

mushrooms (not sliced!) (you'll need 1 cup)

2 heads romaine lettuce

1 10-ounce bag spinach

**lc 2–3 heads lettuce (*not* iceberg) (3 meals)

**lc 1 head cauliflower (1 meal)

**lc broccoli (1 meal)

**lc zucchini (1 meal)

**lc yellow squash (1 meal)

**lc salad veggies (3 meals)

**red potatoes (1 meal)

**russet potatoes (1 meal)


**CANNED GOODS**

1 14½-ounce can diced tomatoes with roasted garlic and
  onions

1 jar salsa

1 can black olives (garnish)

**1 can black beans (1 meal)


**SPICES**

cumin

nutmeg

oregano

white pepper

**DAIRY/DAIRY CASE**

low-fat sour cream (garnish)

half-and-half (you'll need ½ cup)

blue cheese crumbles (you'll need ⅓ cup)

Parmesan cheese—optional

3 eggs (you'll need to hard-boil 2 eggs)

**lc 8-ounce package cream cheese

**DRY GOODS**

seasoned bread crumbs (2 tablespoons)

**1 pound brown rice

**BAKERY**

**lc low-carb corn tortillas

**whole-grain rolls

**corn tortillas

**OTHER**

bamboo or metal skewers

# BARBECUED LEMON CHICKEN

*Serves 4*

*½ cup lemon juice*
*2 tablespoons olive oil*
*4 cloves garlic, pressed*
*Salt and pepper to taste*
*4 boneless, skinless chicken breast halves*

In a zipper-topped plastic bag, place everything but the chicken and mush around. Now add the chicken and, again, mush around to coat completely. Place bag in the fridge for up to an hour, while you get the rest of dinner together. If you are following the LC Serving Suggestion, soak your bamboo skewers for at least 30 minutes before grilling to prevent them from igniting.

Preheat outside grill or grilling appliance, or if you are using the broiler, preheat the broiler to about medium-high heat. Place the chicken on the grill and cook for about 5 minutes or so per side, depending on the thickness of the chicken.

**PER SERVING**
202 Calories; 8g Fat (37.2% calories from fat); 28g Protein; 4g Carbohydrate; trace Dietary Fiber; 68mg Cholesterol; 78mg Sodium. Exchanges: 4 Lean Meat; 0 Vegetable; 0 Fruit; 1½ Fat.

**LC SERVING SUGGESTION:** Serve with grilled zucchini, yellow squash, onion, and tomato kabobs.

**SERVING SUGGESTION:** Add red potatoes.

**DO-AHEAD TIP:** Grill 3 extra chicken breasts for tomorrow night's dinner.

# COBB SALAD

*1 head romaine lettuce, chopped*
*3 boneless, skinless chicken breast halves, cooked and chopped*
*4 slices turkey bacon, cooked and chopped*
*1 avocado, cubed*
*1 tomato, diced*
*⅓ cup blue cheese, crumbled*
*2 eggs, hard-boiled and diced*
*4 tablespoons vinaigrette, homemade or bottled—your choice*

Throw all ingredients into a large bowl, toss with the dressing, divvy up onto 4 plates, and serve. How easy was that!

PER SERVING
395 Calories; 26g Fat (57.0% calories from fat); 33g Protein; 11g Carbohydrate; 5g Dietary Fiber; 178mg Cholesterol; 453mg Sodium. Exchanges: 4 Lean Meat; 1½ Vegetable; 0 Fruit; 4 Fat.

LC SERVING SUGGESTION: This salad stands alone. You don't need anything else.

SERVING SUGGESTION: Add whole-grain rolls.

# UNSHISHED KABOBS

*Serves 4*

*⅓ cup teriyaki sauce*

*1 tablespoon rice vinegar*

*½ tablespoon sesame oil*

*1 pound sirloin steak, trimmed and cut in strips*

*1 tablespoon vegetable oil*

*1½ cups red and green bell pepper, cut in strips*

*1 onion, chopped*

*1 cup mushrooms, quartered*

In a large, zipper-topped plastic bag, place the teriyaki, rice vinegar, and sesame oil. Add the beef and mush around. Place bag in the fridge while you prepare the vegetables and side dishes.

In a skillet, heat the oil over medium-high heat. Stir-fry the veggies all together till tender, about 3 to 5 minutes. Remove the veggies and keep warm.

Now drain the beef and add the beef to the skillet, cooking to your desired doneness, about 5 minutes for medium rare. Add back the vegetables and cook till all is warmed, and serve.

PER SERVING
325 Calories; 21g Fat (57.9% calories from fat); 23g Protein; 11g Carbohydrate; 2g Dietary Fiber; 71mg Cholesterol; 981mg Sodium. Exchanges: 3 Lean Meat; 2 Vegetable; 2½ Fat; 0 Other Carbohydrates.

LC SERVING SUGGESTION: Serve with a big green salad.

SERVING SUGGESTION: Add brown rice.

# WAHOO TACOS

*4 fish fillets, cooked (broil fish or cook however you like; you need
    cooked fish to start)*
*8 romaine lettuce leaves (nice big ones; these are your wraps) (chop
    the remaining head of romaine to be used in the taco)*
*1 cup cilantro, finely chopped*
*Salsa—your choice*

*Lime wedges*
*Chilies*
*Black olives*
*Low-fat sour cream*

### GUACAMOLE
*1 ripe avocado, cubed*
*1 tomato, diced*
*1 small red onion, finely chopped*
*1 clove garlic, pressed*
*1 teaspoon cumin*
*¼ teaspoon oregano*
*Salt and pepper to taste*
*Juice of 1–2 limes, depending how you like it*

To make the guacamole: Mix all ingredients and chill. Throw the
seed in the middle to keep it from turning brown while you prepare the
taco plates.

On each plate, first place a romaine lettuce leaf and spread the fish,
then the chopped lettuce, then the cilantro. Serve with guacamole and
salsa on the side. Place small bowls of the garnishes on the table, too,
for everyone to use. Serve and enjoy!

**PER SERVING**
301 Calories; 10g Fat (28.3% calories from fat); 44g Protein; 11g Carbohydrate; 4g Dietary
Fiber; 99mg Cholesterol; 140mg Sodium. Exchanges: 0 Grain (Starch); 5½ Lean Meat; 1 Vegetable; 0 Fruit; 1½ Fat.

**LC SERVING SUGGESTIONS:** Serve with low-carb corn tortillas instead of the romaine leaves if you like. Add a big green salad.

**SERVING SUGGESTIONS:** Add real corn tortillas and some black beans.

# RATATOUILLE TURKEY

2 tablespoons olive oil
8 turkey breast cutlets
1 cup green pepper strips
1 onion, chopped
1 cup diced eggplant
1 cup sliced zucchini
1 14½-ounce can diced tomatoes with roasted garlic and onions
1 10-ounce bag spinach
Grated Parmesan cheese—optional

In a large saucepan over medium-high heat, heat oil; add turkey and green pepper strips. Cook, stirring frequently, till turkey is just opaque, but not quite cooked through.

Add the onion, eggplant, and zucchini; cook 3 minutes more, stirring frequently, or until vegetables are tender.

Stir in the diced tomatoes; heat to boiling. Reduce heat; simmer till all is warmed.

Meanwhile, place a large handful (about 1 cup) of spinach on each plate. Serve the turkey mixture on top, allowing the heat from the turkey to wilt the spinach perfectly. Garnish with grated Parmesan if desired.

**PER SERVING**
273 Calories; 9g Fat (30.1% calories from fat); 38g Protein; 11g Carbohydrate; 4g Dietary Fiber; 90mg Cholesterol; 383mg Sodium. Exchanges: 5 Lean Meat; 2 Vegetable; 1½ Fat.

**LC SERVING SUGGESTION:** Serve with a green salad as well.

**SERVING SUGGESTIONS:** Serve on brown rice instead, and have the spinach on the side, very lightly steamed.

# CROCK LOAF

*Serves 4*

> 1½ *pounds ground turkey*
> 1 *onion, chopped*
> 1 *stalk celery, chopped*
> 3 *cloves garlic, pressed*
> ½ *cup half-and-half*
> 1 *egg*
> 1 *teaspoon cumin*
> ½ *teaspoon nutmeg*
> ⅛ *teaspoon white pepper*
> 2 *tablespoons seasoned bread crumbs*
> 2 *tablespoons ketchup*

Lightly grease your crock.

In a large mixing bowl, throw in all the ingredients. Using very *clean hands*, mix together well the meat and the rest of the ingredients. Form a little loaf that will fit nicely into your Crock-Pot.

Cover and cook on low for about 8 hours or so, depending on the type of slow cooker you have.

**PER SERVING**
350 Calories; 19g Fat (49.7% calories from fat); 33g Protein; 10g Carbohydrate; 1g Dietary Fiber; 192mg Cholesterol; 385mg Sodium. Exchanges: 0 Grain (Starch); 4½ Lean Meat; ½ Vegetable; 0 Non-Fat Milk; 1 Fat; 0 Other Carbohydrates.

**LC SERVING SUGGESTIONS:** Serve with Mashed Faux-tay-toes (page 246) and steamed broccoli.

**SERVING SUGGESTION:** Add real mashed potatoes.

# SERVING SUGGESTION RECIPES

I'm a big believer in nonrecipes for side dishes. I don't have the time for recipes for side dishes, and I bet you don't either. But you are welcome to use these recipes however they may help you to make your own side dishes, either as inspiration or as exact instructions. Either way, I wanted you to have side dishes and veggies to go with your entrées.

In the first *Saving Dinner*, I was able to organize things much more seasonally than was possible in this book. Unfortunately, when it comes to low-carb veggies, the pickin's are somewhat more slim. So I use anything I can veggie-wise, all year round, for the sake of variety.

## CAULIFLOWER

The most wonderful thing to happen to a low-carber is the rediscovery of the cauliflower. Able to substitute for potatoes in any given recipe, these luscious stand-ins for taters do a cook proud and help take the edge off the hankering for a big pile of mashed potatoes.

Here is a series of cauliflower recipes that will soothe your potato passion and wake up a tender love you never knew you had for this plain Jane, cruciferous veggie.

# MASHED FAUX-TAY-TOES

*Serves 4*

*1 head cauliflower, about 1 pound*
*3 tablespoons cream cheese*
*Salt and pepper to taste*

Wash the cauliflower, peel off any leaves, and trim down the stem. Place the head in a pan containing about 2 inches of water. Place the pan on high heat and bring to a boil, lower the temperature to about medium, cover the pan, and cook till cauliflower is fork tender, about 10 minutes or so.

Drain well and add cream cheese and salt and pepper to taste. Using a potato masher, mash the way you would mash potatoes, and serve when you get the desired consistency.

### PER SERVING
66 Calories; 4g Fat (49.5% calories from fat); 3g Protein; 6g Carbohydrate; 3g Dietary Fiber; 12mg Cholesterol; 66mg Sodium. Exchanges: 0 Lean Meat; 1 Vegetable; ½ Fat.


# SPICED CAULIFLOWER

*Serves 4*

*1 head cauliflower, steamed and cut into pieces, about 1 pound*
*1 tablespoon olive oil*
*½ teaspoon cumin*
*½ teaspoon garlic powder*
*Salt and pepper to taste*

Preheat oven to 400 degrees F.

In a bowl, toss together the hot, steamed cauliflower, oil, spices, and salt and pepper to taste.

Place in a baking dish and bake for 10 to 15 minutes or until lightly browned on top.

### PER SERVING
60 Calories; 4g Fat (48.9% calories from fat); 2g Protein; 6g Carbohydrate; 3g Dietary Fiber; 0mg Cholesterol; 35mg Sodium. Exchanges: 0 Grain (Starch); 0 Lean Meat; 1 Vegetable; ½ Fat.

# BAKED CHEESY CAULIFLOWER

*Serves 4*

    1 head cauliflower, steamed whole, about 1 pound
    1 tablespoon butter
    ½ tablespoon Dijon mustard
    ½ cup low-fat Cheddar cheese

Preheat oven to 400 degrees F.

Place the hot steamy head of cauliflower in a baking dish. Rub the butter over the top evenly. Then brush on the mustard. Now cover the top with the cheese.

Bake for 10 to 15 minutes or until cheese is hot and bubbly.

PER SERVING
80 Calories; 4g Fat (43.8% calories from fat); 6g Protein; 6g Carbohydrate; 3g Dietary Fiber; 11mg Cholesterol; 173mg Sodium. Exchanges: ½ Lean Meat; 1 Vegetable; ½ Fat; 0 Other Carbohydrates.

# FAUX-TAY-TOE SALAD

*Serves 4*

    1 pound cauliflower, steamed
    ½ onion, chopped fine
    3 tablespoons mayonnaise
    ½ tablespoon relish
    2 eggs, hard-boiled, chopped
    2 green onions, minced
    Salt and pepper to taste

In a bowl, mix everything together, and season with salt and pepper to taste. Cover and refrigerate for a few hours for best flavor.

PER SERVING
151 Calories; 12g Fat (64.6% calories from fat); 6g Protein; 9g Carbohydrate; 3g Dietary Fiber; 110mg Cholesterol; 141mg Sodium. Exchanges: ½ Lean Meat; 1½ Vegetable; 1 Fat; 0 Other Carbohydrates.

# TURNIPS AND RUTABAGAS

Turnips and rutabagas are also wonderful substitutes for potatoes and make great fries and oven-roasted veggies. They aren't as low in carbs as cauliflower, but they beat the eyes off a potato any day in a comparative-carb contest. No doubt your initial reaction to such underground underdogs is that you wish they would stay underground. All I ask is that you give them a chance, to almost quote John Lennon.

Work with me a little and let's get adventurous. Together, we'll dig the dirt and root for these marvelous veggies. Ladies and gentlemen, give it up for turnips and rutabagas!

## TURNIP FRIES

*Serves 4*

*4 turnips, cut into steak fries*
*1 tablespoon olive oil*
*½ teaspoon garlic powder*
*Salt and pepper to taste*

Preheat oven to 425 degrees F.

In a bowl, toss together the turnips, olive oil, garlic powder, and salt and pepper to taste.

Lay pieces out on a cookie sheet or jelly-roll pan, not touching. Bake for about 15 to 20 minutes on one side till browned; turn over and bake for another 15 to 20 minutes on the other side. Fries are done when tender on the inside and nicely browned on the outside.

**PER SERVING**
64 Calories; 3g Fat (46.6% calories from fat); 1g Protein; 8g Carbohydrate; 2g Dietary Fiber; 0mg Cholesterol; 82mg Sodium. Exchanges: 0 Grain (Starch); 1½ Vegetable; ½ Fat.

To make Oven-Roasted Turnips, cut into quarters and add ½ teaspoon thyme when tossing.

# RUTABAGA FRIES

*Serves 4*

*4 rutabagas, cut into steak fries*
*1 tablespoon olive oil*
*½ teaspoon garlic powder*
*Salt and pepper to taste*

Preheat oven to 425 degrees F.

In a bowl, toss together the rutabagas, olive oil, garlic powder, and salt and pepper to taste.

Lay pieces out on a cookie sheet or jelly-roll pan, not touching. Bake for about 15 to 20 minutes on one side till browned; turn over and bake for another 15 to 20 minutes on the other side. Fries are done when tender on the inside and nicely browned on the outside.

**PER SERVING**
81 Calories; 4g Fat (38.1% calories from fat); 2g Protein; 12g Carbohydrate; 4g Dietary Fiber; 0mg Cholesterol; 28mg Sodium. Exchanges: ½ Grain (Starch); ½ Fat.

To make Mashed Rutabagas, steam peeled rutabagas and follow the same directions for Mashed Faux-tay-toes, using rutabagas.

To make Oven-Roasted Rutabagas, cut into quarters and add ½ teaspoon thyme when tossing.

To make Real Oven Fries for the non-low-carbers in your household, follow the same directions as above using potatoes.


## SPAGHETTI SQUASH

Spaghetti squash is the obvious stand-in for pasta. It won't exactly fool you into believing the squash strands entering your mouth are actually angel hair pasta, but it's close enough to be enjoyed and used as a bed for some of the saucier low-carb entrées.

Baking a spaghetti squash can take a good long time, and one of my recommendations is to prebake them whole and deal with them later when it's cooking time. To do so, just stab the thing a couple of times, throw it directly on the rack of a preheated 350-degree F oven, and allow it to cook till softened. Then cool and refrigerate till you want to use it. The very idea of trying to split a hard squash horizontally is enough of a fright to make me want to dial 911 as a precaution. If you have tried this before, you know what I mean. Severing an artery is a very real hazard to such foolishness.

I have seen tips that suggest you open a hard squash with a cleaver and mallet. I am not saying this can't be done, but if I have to go digging through tool boxes to make dinner happen, well, no. Uh-uh. I like my method better.

Here's a bit of a recipe, too, although you could just prebake, open it up, deseed it, pull out the strands with a fork, and heat them up. Still, the following idea will make spaghetti squash a bit tastier:

## SPAGHETTI SQUASH ROMANO

*Serves 4*

*1 pound spaghetti squash, prebaked*
*1 tablespoon butter*
*Salt and pepper to taste*
*¼ cup Romano cheese, grated*

Once you have prebaked your squash, split it open horizontally and deseed and degoop it. Then, using a fork, pull the strings out of the squash. Set aside.

In a saucepan, melt your butter. Add the strings and toss, salting and peppering liberally. Serve with the Romano cheese on top.

PER SERVING
88 Calories; 5g Fat (52.3% calories from fat); 3g Protein; 8g Carbohydrate; 1g Dietary Fiber; 15mg Cholesterol; 133mg Sodium. Exchanges: ½ Lean Meat; 1½ Vegetable; 1 Fat.

## TO STEAM OR NOT TO STEAM? 'TIS NOBLER TO SAUTÉ . . .

I often get questions from subscribers asking me how to steam or sauté their veggies. Here is some help on both methods.

### To Steam

This is a very quick, easy method to get your veggies on the table fast without losing precious nutrients. First off, you need to cut your veggies up into uniform-size pieces. This helps with even cooking. Second, use an inexpensive steamer basket that fits into your saucepan to allow the steam to do its job. If you don't have a steamer, just place your veggies in a shallow pan with about an inch of water and boil/steam them to desired consistency. (This is called faking it—it is not the end of the world if you don't have a steamer.) Cooking time will vary, depending on what you're steaming.

You want the vegetables to be tender, not mushy. They should still be pretty to look at, too, not an awful pea-green-soup color. You'll know you've gone too far if they look like that.

### Or Not to Steam: The Great Sauté

I am particularly enthusiastic about sautéing my veggies, particularly green beans. If you're in a hurry, you can cut some of the sauté time by steaming your green beans first, then heading to the skillet. Or you can sauté them from beginning to end—my only recommendation is that you cut them on a diagonal (French-cut) to help speed along the process.

And while the word *sauté* may be French, the act of sautéing, especially veggies, is more effectively done with the Asian method of wokking your veggies in your flat-bottomed wok (if you're as blessed as I am and you own one). The higher sides, the high heat, and the constant stirring and tossing in the hot oil help to tenderize the veggies by evaporating their water and caramelizing them at the same time. The savory result is delicious, better-tasting veggies. Add some garlic, salt and pepper, and perhaps an herb or two, and you have restaurant-quality side dishes.

In this book, I've suggested sautéed green beans more than once, and I've also mentioned green beans sautéed together with portobello mushrooms. The only thing to remember when doing mixed sautéed veggies is to sauté the harder, longer-cooking one first, then add the other one toward the end. So the green beans would go in first, then toward the end of the cooking time, the portobello slices would be added. Cinchy!

# PUMPKIN PATCH

Eating by color, as previously explained in *Saving Dinner,* is one of the ways to obtain optimal nutrition. The bright orange color of pumpkin is a screaming advertisement for the beta-carotene lurking within. Beta-carotene is responsible for helping to fight off cancer, boosting your immune system, and giving your heart some protection against heart disease.

Unfortunately, most winter squashes are loaded not only with beta-carotene, but with lots of carbs, too. For example, as healthy as a sweet potato is, it still carries a whopping 12 grams of carbs for half a medium baked sweet potato. Yikes! In the scheme of things, that's a bit over the top for a carb watcher. You can get the same rich flavor and the same hit on beta-carotene eating pumpkin. So try this recipe. You will see for yourself pumpkin isn't just for pies anymore.

## BAKED PUMPKIN WEDGES

*Serves 4*

> 4 pieces pumpkin (use the little pie pumpkins, also known as sugar
>    pumpkins)
> 1 tablespoon olive oil
> Salt and pepper to taste
> ¼ teaspoon nutmeg

Preheat the oven to 425 degrees F.

Lightly oil the pumpkin on the fleshy side, salt and pepper to taste, then sprinkle nutmeg.

Bake for about 30 minutes or until the pumpkin is tender.

**PER SERVING**
61 Calories; 4g Fat (47.6% calories from fat); 1g Protein; 8g Carbohydrate; 1g Dietary Fiber; 0mg Cholesterol; 1mg Sodium. Exchanges: ½ Grain (Starch); ½ Fat.

# PUMPKIN PUREE

*Serves 4*

*2 cups pumpkin, boiled*
*1 tablespoon butter*
*2 tablespoons half-and-half*
*Salt and pepper to taste*
*Nutmeg to taste*

Cut the pumpkin open, deseed, and then peel and cut the pumpkin into 2-inch pieces. Place the pieces in a pan, cover with water, and simmer till fork tender.

Drain the pumpkin. To the hot pumpkin, add remaining ingredients, except nutmeg. Mash with a potato masher till smooth.

Serve the puree and top with a little nutmeg.

**PER SERVING**
50 Calories; 4g Fat (63.4% calories from fat); 1g Protein; 4g Carbohydrate; trace Dietary Fiber; 11mg Cholesterol; 33mg Sodium. Exchanges: 0 Grain (Starch); 0 Non-Fat Milk; 1 Fat.

# SAUTÉED GARLICKY SPINACH

*Serves 4*

This might seem like a lot of spinach; just remember that you get a ton of shrinkage when you're dealing with spinach.

*1 10-ounce bag spinach, preferably baby spinach, if available*
*1 tablespoon olive oil*
*2 cloves garlic, pressed*
*Salt and pepper to taste*

In a large skillet, heat the olive oil over medium-high heat. Add the garlic and sauté for just a minute, making sure not to let it get brown.

Add half the spinach and sauté for a minute. It will shrink up, giving you room to add the other half. Keep sautéing until you get the desired doneness. Personally, I like it barely cooked, so making this takes me all of 2 minutes.

**PER SERVING**
48 Calories; 4g Fat (61.6% calories from fat); 2g Protein; 3g Carbohydrate; 2g Dietary Fiber; 0mg Cholesterol; 56mg Sodium. Exchanges: ½ Vegetable; ½ Fat.

## BALSAMIC VINAIGRETTE

*Makes 1 cup*

1 tablespoon Dijon mustard
4 tablespoons balsamic vinegar
1 teaspoon sugar
¼ cup olive oil
Salt and pepper to taste

Throw all ingredients in a jar and shake it so hard you feel your eyeballs banging around in their sockets.

VARIATION: Like garlic? We must be related. Throw 1 clove of pressed garlic (or 2 if you need to ward off vampires) in for good measure. Keep shaking!

# BASIC COLESLAW

*Serves 4*

*½ bag coleslaw mix from the produce department*
*1½ tablespoons mayonnaise, more or less*
*Splash rice vinegar (may also be called rice wine vinegar)*

Mix the whole kit and caboodle together. That's it.

I am guessing on everything as far as amounts go. I just throw it in a bowl and go. It's one of those multitasking-type recipes—you make it while grilling food, talking to your mother on the phone, and feeding the dog—all without missing a beat.

**PER SERVING**
Roughly around 5 grams of fat and 2 net grams carbs.

**VARIATION: ASIAN SLAW**

Reduce the mayo to 1 tablespoon, and add ½ tablespoon of sesame oil and about ½ cup chopped cilantro. Garnish with some crushed dry-roasted peanuts, if desired.

# SPINACH QUESADILLAS

*Serves 4*

When you make quesadillas, remember it's like making grilled cheese sandwiches. Easy!

*1 tablespoon olive oil, divided*
*4 large whole-wheat-flour tortillas*
*1⅓ cups low-fat Cheddar cheese*
*4 cups fresh spinach*

In a skillet, heat a bit of the olive oil. You are going to make these in batches.

Add the tortilla, laying it flat. Now add a little cheese, then the spinach, then the cheese. Cook over medium-high heat. When the spinach starts to wilt and the cheese to melt, fold over in half and press down. Flip it over and cook for another minute. You will be able to tell when they are done. Repeat this process till all the quesadillas are made.

**PER SERVING**
336 Calories; 11g Fat (30.3% calories from fat); 16g Protein; 42g Carbohydrate; 3g Dietary Fiber; 8mg Cholesterol; 598mg Sodium. Exchanges: 2½ Grain (Starch); 1½ Lean Meat; 0 Vegetable; 1½ Fat.

**VARIATION: PLAIN QUESADILLAS**
To make a plain quesadilla, skip the spinach. Or try your own variation by adding any ingredients that suit your fancy.

**VARIATION: LOW-CARB**
Use La Tortilla Factory low-carb tortillas to bring the carb count *way* down.

## TORTILLA CHIPS

*Serves 4*

Preheat oven to 400 degrees F.

Stack 4 low-carb corn tortillas and cut into eighths. Brush or spray with oil.

Place the tortillas on a cookie sheet without touching and cook till crisp, about 5 minutes. Watch them . . . they can overcook easily.

## CAPRICE SALAD

*Serves 4*

*2 tomatoes, sliced*
*1 bunch basil leaves*
*8 ounces part-skim mozzarella cheese, fresh if available*
*1 tablespoon olive oil*

On a large plate, alternate slices of tomato, basil leaf, and mozzarella until you make a complete circle of red, green, and white with the ingredients. Drizzle the top with the olive oil and let everyone serve himself.

PER SERVING
202 Calories; 13g Fat (59.0% calories from fat); 16g Protein; 5g Carbohydrate; 1g Dietary Fiber; 31mg Cholesterol; 305mg Sodium. Exchanges: 2 Lean Meat; ½ Vegetable; 1½ Fat.

# INDEX

## ABOUT THE AUTHOR

LEANNE ELY is considered *the* expert on family cooking and healthy eating. She is a certified nutritionist, public speaker, and the host of Savingdinner.com. She has a weekly "Food for Thought" column on the ever-popular Flylady.net website, as well as her own e-zine, Healthy Foods, which has been published weekly for the past four years. She lives in North Carolina with her two teenaged children.

## ABOUT THE TYPE

This book was set in Goudy, a typeface designed by Frederic William Goudy (1865–1947). Goudy began his career as a bookkeeper, but devoted the rest of his life to the pursuit of "recognized quality" in a printing type.

Goudy was produced in 1914 and was an instant bestseller for the foundry. It has generous curves and smooth, even color. It is regarded as one of Goudy's finest achievements.